you and y_____
co____

PUPPY

in a
nutshell

The essential owners' guide to perfect puppy
parenting – with easy-to-follow steps on how
to choose and care for your new Cockapoo

Carry Aylward

NUTSHELL
BOOKS

www.nutshell-books.com

ISBN: 978-1-8384748-0-5

Front cover design by Nutshell Books
Book design by Nutshell Books
Photography: Tim McNeil, © AdobeStock,
Debbie McNeil, © Shutterstock, © iStock, Jon Hulett

Printed by Kindle Direct Publishing

First printed 2021

Nutshell Books
3 Holmlea Road, Goring on Thames
RG8 9EX, United Kingdom
www.nutshell-books.com

For you, the reader, for wanting to be a great owner, and for the super-special Cockapoo you bring into your heart and home

CONTENTS

Foreword 7

1. Are you ready? 9
   - Is a Cockapoo right for you? 12

2. What makes a Cockapoo? 17
   - The three Cocker Spaniels 19
   - The three Poodles 21
   - How do we apply this? 22
   - The 'F' numbers explained 23
   - What is a 'true' Cockapoo? 24

3. Finding the litter 26
   - Decide what you're looking for 26
   - Timing 30
   - The breeder 31

4. Buying responsibly 32

5. The paperwork 39

6. Which puppy? 42

7. Preparing for the big day 47

8. Picking up your puppy 54

9. The homecoming 58

10. New puppy safety 61

11. The first night 66

12. The first week 69

13. Emotional development 75
    - Fragile! Handle with care 75
    - Socialisation 76
    - Habituation 77
    - Time alone 79
    - Barking 80

    - Aggression 80

    - Small children 80

    - Further crate training 82

    - Eating poo – seriously? 82

14. Essential care 85

    - Feeding 86

    - Grooming 90

15. Behaviour 97

16. Toilet training 104

17. Chewing house and home 108

18. Mouthing and nipping 111

19. Jumping up 113

20. Digging 115

21. Barking 117

22. Separation anxiety 121

23. Stepping out 125

24. Exercise 130

25. Training 136

    - Calling to you 139

    - 'Sit' 141

    - 'Down' 142

    - 'Stay' 143

26. Playtime! 145

    - Games 146

    - Toys 149

27. Travelling by car 151

28. Puppy-people translator 153

29. Adolescence 157

    - Neutering 158

30. Going forward 161

31. There will be times 165

32. Useful contacts 168

Index 169

FOREWORD

You're considering a puppy, and more specifically a Cockapoo. Of course you are, given their teddy-bear appeal, rubber-ball bounce and overwhelming affection for one and all. Oodles and Doodles have become hugely popular in the past two decades and with good reason. And Cockapoos in particular are literally bounding into the hearts and homes of families everywhere – rendering their humans loopy with love.

Whether you've already brought your puppy home, or you're still weighing up the pros and cons of this hugely popular crossbreed, I am thrilled for you. Congratulations on taking this step towards being an excellent owner because, while Cockapoos **will** steal your heart, there **will** also be times when they'll have you pulling your hair out – they are hugely energetic, want to be with you all the time, and can be easily bored. They will get wet and muddy given the chance, and they will need regular brushing and clipping.

A deliberate, designer cross between a Cocker Spaniel and a Poodle, Cockapoos are also known by other hybrid-style names, Spoodles in Australia, for example, and Cockadoodles in Sweden. The spelling takes on different forms too, common variations being Cock-A-Poos and Cockerdoodles, but in these pages I will refer to them as Cockapoos.

Whether or not you've owned a Spaniel, a Poodle, or indeed any dog before, you've chosen the ideal starter guide for Cockapoo puppy parents-to-be. This book answers the most important early-stage questions and leads you step by step through the entire process, from deciding whether a Cockapoo is in fact the best choice for you, through the first days, to the subsequent weeks and months – that all-important formative time when your puppy is growing and learning at its fastest, and when you need to put the most energy into its upbringing and training.

It is intentionally concise, bringing together up-to-date research in an easy-to-read, easy-to-follow format that gives you only what you need to know, when you need to know it.

At times your puppy is referred to as 'he' and at other times as 'she', but please consider both 'he' and 'she' to mean 'he or she' in every suitable instance.

The advice in this book will help you to build a solid foundation for a wonderful relationship with your Cockapoo. It is meant to keep you smiling not only through the love and cuddles, but also through the puddles and poops, heart-wrenching nights and shredded items of value.

All you need now is to brace yourself with unconditional love and a good sense of humour, and let's get started.

I. ARE YOU READY?

Along with their bounding energy, Cockapoos have kind and gentle natures which make them a good choice for most people, including first-time dog owners. They are low-shedding, extremely adaptable and can make wonderful companions. But before we delve into the specifics of their characteristics, and how to raise and care for a Cockapoo, let's run through some quick but important questions. Choosing a dog is a momentous, life-changing and long-term decision, so if

you're undecided about a puppy, and more specifically a Cockapoo, this chapter will help you to make a more informed decision.

If you are new to owning a dog, any dog, when you invite one into your world, your life will never be the same. You will soon start thinking differently about what you wear, the places you visit, your holiday destinations and possibly even the car you drive. Your life will also be warmer, messier, happier and richer in so many ways.

But are you really ready for a dog?

If you invite a dog into your home, she should be treated like family. Ask yourself very honestly whether, at this time in your life, and for the next 12 to 15 years or longer, you will be able to give her the love, care, time, exercise, training and patience she deserves.

Is a puppy right for you?

Ask yourself honestly whether you can face the puppy stage with the pooping, weeing and chewing of everything in sight. An adolescent Cockapoo can be a real handful – right until around two years of age – and needs a huge amount of training and socialising. Ask yourself whether you have the time and energy. If not, you might consider taking on an older dog. An adult that needs rehoming will have finished with toilet training, teething and even adolescence.

Another option is to give a home to a dog in its senior years. There are so many beautiful older dogs that need re-homing through no fault of their own, so if you are no longer as strong or active as you once were, this might be the best choice for you now.

Do you have other pets?

If you have other pets, consider carefully how a new dog would fit in to your family. If you choose a Cockapoo puppy and socialise it well, there's no reason for her to have a problem with your existing pets. Your existing pets, however, might not be quite so adaptable.

You still want a puppy?

I know. They're warm and cuddly and there's nothing as sweet as the pitter patter of puppy feet. But please note: the first steps to getting a puppy are a big investment – not just financially, but also in terms of time, energy and emotion. This is not an attempt to put you off getting a dog. Quite the opposite. It's just really important that you are sure you are able to give your puppy the happy life it deserves and fully understand the commitment you're making. Too many dogs are re-homed and even put down each year because their owners underestimated the responsibility.

And be sure to involve any other members of the household in this decision. It's very important that everyone has bought into the whole idea from the very start. The more say the family has in owning a dog, choosing the breed, and choosing your specific puppy, the more likely they will be to actively engage with and care for it, and the less likely they'll be to shirk their dog-walking, poo-picking responsibilities.

So if you're sure you can give your dog the love, time, care and attention she needs and deserves, and you're sure a puppy is the way forward, **and** you're brave enough to let those four extra feet bound freely through your heart and home, then let's take a closer look at what to expect from a Cockapoo.

IS A COCKAPOO RIGHT FOR YOU?

Wherever you are in your puppy-finding journey, even if you've already brought your special puppy home, it's still useful to know the traits and characteristics you're likely to encounter in a Cockapoo.

These are more difficult to predict with a crossbreed than with a purebred where both parents are of the same breed. But we can start by looking at traits that are common to both sides of the ancestry. For example, with Cocker Spaniel and Poodle in their make up, you can be pretty sure that, no matter which parent the puppies takes after, they will be playful, energetic, intelligent and people loving.

The following is a fuller summary of the key characteristics you can expect in a Cockapoo. They are not necessarily good or bad in themselves, they are simply more or less right for you and your circumstances. The first two qualities listed below are especially important, not because they are the most prevalent, but because they are the ones that most often take new owners by surprise.

Need company

Cockapoos want to be with their humans **all the time**. They are very sociable, and consequently prone to separation anxiety if left on their own for long stretches. Don't get one if you're going to be out at work all day.

High energy levels

They're energetic and can be over-bouncy. Considering both parent breeds are working dogs this is not surprising. They might look like cuddly teddies, but don't be fooled into thinking they'll lounge around.

While they make great indoor dogs, and they'll try their furry paws at being lapdogs from time to time, they're lively and enthusiastic and need lots of attention. They must get regular exercise and all the exercise they need, and that is usually a good one to two hours a day. A short walk around the block isn't enough for a Cockapoo, especially if its Spaniel ancestry is working Cocker (see 'The Three Cocker Spaniels' in Chapter 2).

Need outside time

They also need regular access to the outdoors. Cockapoos can be housed anywhere from an apartment to a farm, but they love little more than running freely off the lead and they absolutely must have daily opportunities to race about outside, come rain, shine or even snow. They adore snow. And they usually love water too, especially from the Poodle side of their breeding.

Appealing

There is precious little cuter than a Cockapoo puppy. No matter how they're mixed, those wide, expressive eyes on endearing teddy faces will pull at your heartstrings, and the silk-shaggy coats will call on you to reach out and stroke them.

Their sweet natures make them every bit as adorable. Well-raised Cockapoos are:
- friendly with everyone
- bouncy, happy, enthusiastic and optimistic
- playful and fun
- mischievous and quirky
- loving and loyal
- sensitive, kind and gentle
- eager to please and willing.

Practical

Cockapoos are good with people of all ages – they're great with children, and usually get on with other dogs too. Being small-to-medium in height and weight, they're a manageable size without being fragile. The Poodle coat in their make-up is low-shedding and clean. They make outstanding all-round family pets and are a sensible choice for inexperienced owners.

Adaptable

Unlike many breeds that bond most closely with one person, Cockapoos often bond with the whole family. What's more, the Cocker Spaniel in them adapts quickly to new surroundings. One minute they can be racing around in circles, and the next they can be draped over your favourite armchair like an expensive throw.

Intelligent

They're intelligent, albeit with a streak of madness, and love playtimes and a mental challenge. Combined with their eagerness to please, this makes them easier to train than the average breed; toilet training included. But it also means they can quickly get bored.

Sensitive

They are also highly intuitive and will pick up on and react to your moods. In fact, their ability to show empathy, together with their intelligence and caring, forgiving natures, make them excellent hearing dogs for the deaf, as well as therapy dogs for the elderly and children, especially those with autism. It does, however, mean that they don't respond well to rough treatment, and they don't always cope well in a stressful environment.

Need mental stimulation

Being a cross between two highly intelligent breeds, a Cockapoo needs mental exercise too. Your attention, training, and games that provide mental stimulation are essential to keep them happy and well-balanced. If you can't give them things to do, they will find things on their own – things that might involve redecorating the furniture for instance.

And regular grooming

A Cockapoo's coat will be anything between the standard Poodle curl and sleek Cocker wave, and typically shed very little. But this doesn't make them an easy grooming option. They need regular brushing and clipping too, which, unless you learn to do it yourself, will mean regular trips to the grooming parlour.

Not good as guard dogs

While some Cockapoos might pass as watchdogs, barking when there's someone at the door, as soon as that door's opened they will welcome the person with mad-tail-wagging delight. They are simply too friendly with one and all.

Magnets for water, mud and shrubbery

Many Cockapoos love a good muddy puddle as much as they love to race through the undergrowth collecting up leaves, twigs and burs in their coats. They will grab any opportunity to get soaked – even in the filthiest of pools – then shower you with their wet and often-muddy bounds of affection. If a pristine house is important to you, a Cockapoo might not be the best choice.

Cost

As with all dogs, the expense is a consideration. Cockapoos are not cheap and after buying your puppy, the cost of pet insurance, vets' bills, food, toys and care is no small consideration.

Bottom line

All Cockapoo puppies have the potential to be wonderful companions. But, in spite of all this high praise, they all have the potential to be problem pets too. For example, if they were left locked up for long stretches, they would become 'difficult': barking, digging and chewing things. Of course they would.

But if you're sure you will give your Cockapoo the love and attention she needs and deserves; if you will keep her active and busy – mentally and physically; and if you will give her playtime, toys and walks, you will have love, devotion and entertainment beyond measure. And those soft teddy paws will make big, teddy paw-prints in your heart.

2. WHAT MAKES A COCKAPOO?

This chapter will give you an understanding of your puppy's ancestry. It's not immediately helpful in terms of choosing or looking after your puppy, but it will equip you with a basic sense of what makes up the crossbreed, which in turn will give you a better all-round awareness of your puppy's needs, and the instincts that drive him.

If we wind back a century or two, or even just a few decades, most dog breeds were selectively developed to be hardy, outdoor working dogs: for hunting, retrieving, herding or guarding. Even for racing and fighting. But the role of dogs in our lives is fast changing from working partner to indoor family companion, and in the past few decades, many breeders have shifted their goals accordingly. They have begun aiming instead for dogs with lovely natures – dogs to make excellent companions and healthy household pets, that will both suit a domestic setting and thrive in one.

It is reportedly in America in the 1950s that breeders first looked to the Cocker Spaniel and the Poodle for this new family-friendly mix. And there began the Cockapoo. So for a basic understanding of your chosen cross, let's start with a quick overview of these two parent breeds.

Cocker Spaniels

There are several strains of Spaniel, all of them much-loved. And of all the Spaniels, Cockers are the most popular. In fact, in the UK they usually rank in the top three of the nation's most favoured dog breeds. It's no surprise then that, in striving for an excellent all-round family pet, breeders began looking their way. With their loving natures, sunny dispositions, ever-wagging tails, beautiful silky coats and practical size, they make wonderful companions and family dogs and there's no doubt they are a good choice for people of all ages and lifestyles.

Poodles

These dogs are currently the number one choice for crossbreeds, which is why there are so many -oodles of -poos and -doodles around. There is a huge amount to praise in Poodles, but it is two features in particular that give them this high standing. Firstly, Poodles are considered the most intelligent dogs in the world after the Border Collie. And secondly, they have unique single-layer woollen coats that are extremely low-shedding, and that make them a clean choice for indoor living. No dog breed is fully hypoallergenic, but allergy sufferers tolerate the Poodle coat far better than other breeds.

Overview behind us, let's move to the next level, because there are in fact three types of Cocker Spaniel and three types of Poodle in the Cockapoo's parents and ancestors mix.

THE THREE COCKER SPANIELS

The English Cocker Spaniel comes in two types, the show Cocker and the working Cocker (although the Kennel Club doesn't distinguish between the two), and in addition there is the American Cocker Spaniel (which is simply called the Cocker Spaniel in the US).

'English' show Cocker

The show Cockers are the biggest of the three Cocker Spaniels. They have compact bodies, domed heads and long ears set low on their heads. They also have long, thick and wavy coats that need a considerable amount of grooming. They are less excitable than their 'working' cousins and need less exercise, and as such can be better suited to a quieter family home.

'English' working Cocker

To look at, working Cockers are lighter framed than the 'show' strain, with more pointed faces and proportionately longer legs and bodies. Their ears are smaller, shorter and sit higher on their heads, and their coats are thinner and shorter.

They were bred to flush game birds from the undergrowth, so they have a high physical as well as mental energy drive, and love nothing more that to run around in thick shrub for hours on end. Needless to say they are better suited to an active household with space to run, and could be a real handful for an owner unwilling or unable to give them an outlet for this energy.

'American' Cocker

These Cockers are smaller than their English counterparts. To look at, their muzzles are shorter and they have a more pronounced stop (the dividing 'line' between the muzzle and the skull). Their ears are set low, they have longer and softer coats, their eyes are rounder, and their tails are set slightly higher on their backs. This strain comes in a 'buff' shade, a light brownish yellow that doesn't feature at all in the English strains.

These Cockers also tend to have a lower prey drive, arguably making them easier family pets.

All three types of Cocker Spaniel are happy and enthusiastic, playful, affectionate and eager to please. They all love running around off the lead and nose-surfing through the undergrowth.

THE THREE POODLES

The three types of Poodles are:
- the **Standard**
- the **Miniature**
- and the **Toy**,

although the vast majority of Cockapoos are bred from the Miniature or the Toy.

Size really is the only key difference. Standards are the original Poodle, typically measuring over 15" (38cm) at the shoulder. Miniatures and Toys are essentially smaller versions of the Standard, with Miniatures measuring between 11" and 15" (28-38cm), and Toys measuring less than 10" (25cm).

All three types have the dense curly woollen coats that make them so good for indoor living, and by way of colouring, all three are usually solids, which is to say, all black, all white or all brown.

Poodles were originally bred as working dogs so they can have a strong prey drive. People often think of them as a pampered and be-ribboned pets punctuated by ridiculous pom-poms, but the truth is they were bred as water dogs – the word Poodle tracing back to the German word meaning 'puddle'. These are gundogs, bred for hunting waterbirds from open water as well as marshes and reed banks, and the pom-pom hairdos were in fact functional. The longer hair was for warmth and to protect the joints, while the shaved areas were to help keep them afloat.

So whether Standard, Miniature or Toy, Poodles are all active, athletic and agile. They love running, swimming and playing, and excel at competition. They are highly intelligent and carry themselves proudly, but can be shy or highly strung with it. This makes sensitive handling hugely important.

They are all exceptionally people-oriented which makes them good family pets, but also means they can be prone to separation anxiety. And they're highly intuitive and sensitive to your moods which makes them wonderful companions, but also means they don't always cope well in a stressful environment.

SO HOW DO WE APPLY THIS?

In bringing these much-loved breeds together, the hope is of course to get the best of both – a lovely natured, happy, healthy, low-shedding Cockapoo. But because of the different breed lines, there can be lots of inconsistencies, and even puppies from the same litter can look remarkably different from their siblings. So with a Cockapoo, you should in fact be ready to experience a degree of any of the qualities typical of both breeds.

However, by understanding the types of Cocker Spaniel and Poodle that make up your puppy, you **can** make some assumptions. For example, the puppy of a working Cocker Spaniel and Standard Poodle should be larger and more energetic than the puppy of a show Cocker and Toy Poodle. The physical differences between Cockapoos are most apparent in size, colour and coat, and size is perhaps the one thing you can reasonably predict, because it is largely influenced by the type of Poodle used in the breeding.

THE 'F' NUMBERS EXPLAINED

Cockapoo litters with the greatest variations in appearance and temperament are usually first generation, or F1, meaning one parent is pure Poodle and the other is pure Cocker Spaniel. Further down the generational line, the traits become more established and predictable. So apart from understanding the types of Cocker Spaniel and Poodle used in the breeding of your puppy, it is helpful to know what percentage of each pure breed your puppy carries. If your puppy is 75% Poodle, for example, you can reasonably expect its appearance and behaviour to be largely Poodle.

For this percentage we need to look at the generations involved, or the often mind-boggling 'F' numbers. If you haven't come across the F numbers yet, you soon will, because they are used to describe the generation of a crossbreed.

Here is a brief explanation.

- **F1** – This is the puppy of two pure breeds, so an F1 Cockapoo is 50% Poodle and 50% Cocker Spaniel. F1s have the reputation of being healthier than either of their parent breeds.
- **F2** – This is second generation. It is a mix of two F1 Cockapoos, and is still 50% of each breed.
- **F3** – An F3 Cockapoo is third generation and the puppy of two F2s, etcetera.

This is simplistic of course because one parent might be F1 while the other is F3. In this case the puppies would be F2, because the F number is worked out by adding one to the lowest F number. So if the parents were F2 and F3, for example, the puppies would be F2 + 1, making them F3.

Alternatively, while one parent is an F-number Cockapoo, the other might be pure Cocker Spaniel or pure Poodle. When this is the case, a 'b' (standing for backcross), is added to the F and number, so an F1b might be the puppy of an F1 Cockapoo and a pedigree (or purebred) Poodle, making it 75% Poodle.

At some point the numbers are dropped and the puppies become 'multigenerational'. By this stage, the litters are far more consistent in nature and appearance than their F1 ancestors, with coats that are neither too curly nor too flat and, dare I say it, a 'true' Cockapoo is emerging.

WHAT IS A 'TRUE' COCKAPOO?

The short answer is that there isn't one. Being a crossbreed, Cockapoos are neither purebred nor pedigree; they are not recognised by purebred registries like the Kennel Club; and consequently there is no official breed standard – a list of attributes the Club considers 'ideal' in a breed.

But having been around since the 1950s, they have had time to become a relatively established and trusted hybrid breed. They are recognised by the International Designer Canine Registry (IDCR), and there's no shortage of Cockapoo clubs and societies.

The Cockapoo Club of Great Britain (CCGB) publishes an ethical standard for breeders. This recognises variation in the dogs and gives little importance to consistency. On the other hand, some breeders are actively working to standardise the breed, and the American Cockapoo Club has published a list of the attributes it considers desirable in a Cockapoo. This is a simplified version of the key points.

Overall appearance: Well-proportioned, appearing sturdy and squarely-built, never 'low and long' or 'tall and gangly'. Line of the back is level to slightly sloping.

Size: Adult Cockapoos measuring 10" (25cm) or less at the shoulder are considered Toy size; those measuring 11-14" (28-36cm) are considered Miniatures; and those measuring over 14" (36cm) are regarded as Standards.

Weight: This can vary considerably, but ideally a Toy would weigh under 12 lb (5.5kg), a Miniature 13-20 lb (6-9kg) and a Standard 21 lb (9.5kg) and over.

Expression: Keen, soulful, intelligent and endearing.

Head: 'Carried high and with dignity'.

Eyes: Large, round, well-set and well-spaced. Should be dark brown in colour on dogs with black noses, but can be lighter on dogs with light-coloured noses. Hair obscuring the vision should be cut back.

Ears: Set on higher than the eyes, and hanging fairly close to the head. Never erect. Well feathered.

Tail: Set on line with the back, and carried on this line or higher. Should be wagging when in motion.

Coat: Can be 'tight curly', 'medium curl' or 'flat'. Breeders strive for the medium curl, but all three types are acceptable. Coat should be clipped in a 'teddy-bear' style: 2-3" long all over, including the tail if it is docked. (Tail docking is optional in the US but illegal in the UK.) If the tail is undocked, the tail hair should be left long. Only facial hair can be longer. A Cockapoo should never be shaved.

Movement: A straight free stride rendering it agile, and capable of great speed and endurance.

3. FINDING THE LITTER

You've decided you want a Cockapoo puppy and I'm thrilled for you. There are magical, sock-nicking, chin-licking times ahead. And more love than you could ever imagine. But don't rush off to see the first litter you come across, because it's close to impossible to resist the pleading eyes of a puppy that wants to go home with you. Before you even start looking for new litters, sort out some basic preferences in your own mind. You needn't stick to them, but they'd be a useful guide.

DECIDE WHAT YOU'RE LOOKING FOR

What size are you most comfortable with? What is your favourite coat type? Do you lean towards a certain colouring? Would you prefer a girl or a boy?

Keep an eye out for Cockapoos when you're out and about, talk to their owners, and look at pictures and video clips. Here are some points to consider while you're shaping your preferences.

Size

If size is important to you, then once you know what you're looking for, make sure the Poodle side of the ancestry is a good match.

26

Coat type

Cockapoo coats can be tight and curly, loose and wavy
(the teddy-bear look) or close to smooth – anything
between the average Poodle curl and the straighter
Cocker coat. If you are hoping for tight curls or low
shedding, you'll be looking for a higher percentage of
Poodle in the ancestry. If you prefer the smoother coat,
which is incidentally also easier to care for, then you'd
be safer with more Cocker Spaniel in the mix.

Be warned that just looking at a litter can be
misleading because Cockapoo puppies are **all** born with
soft, wavy coats. Only when they are a few weeks old
can you **start** to get an idea of the coat type, and it is
only around the six-to-nine-month mark that their adult
coats really begin to show. Finding out about the
puppies' ancestry as well as the parents' coat types will
help to give you an idea of what to expect.

Colour and markings

You're spoilt for choice with Cockapoos because they
come in just about every shade and pattern. There is
Brown ranging from Light to Dark and Chocolate; Red
from Apricot to Deep Auburn and Gold; and Cream
from Buff to Champagne. There is White, Black and
Silver. There is Sable (brown hairs turning to black at

the tips) and Roan or Merle (mottled). The colour can be solid, or with a small or large amount of White, or with White and Tan, or a Dilute (a faded take on a solid colour). Markings can include patches, spots and ticking (flecks of colour).

Theories abound linking certain colours and markings to certain characteristics, especially on the Cocker Spaniel side. For example, there is talk of flecks being 'naughty spots'. and of certain of the solid coloured dogs being more eager to please. As far as I can tell, there is nothing but sweeping speculation to suggest that a Cockapoo's temperament can be linked to its colouring. You quite likely already have your favourite or favourites, and whatever you choose will be lovely.

If you have a strong preference for colour, then knowing the colouring of the father as well as the mother can put you on the most likely track, especially if the litter has not yet been born.

It's worth noting that, as with coat types, coat colours can also change. A Cockapoo puppy's shade will often become lighter or darker between puppyhood and adulthood, with a move towards lighter being more common.

Girl or boy?

If you already have another dog, it would be sensible to choose a puppy from the opposite sex to avoid jealousy or competition. That said, if your existing dog is un-neutered, a puppy from the opposite sex mightn't be such a good idea.

But quite honestly, other dogs aside – and if you're not hoping to use him or her for breeding someday – I don't believe there's much in it. Every Cockapoo really is his or her own 'person,' and health and temperament are far more important considerations. Good training and keeping your puppy in its right place in the family 'pack' are much better determining factors in how he or she will turn out and fit into your family.

Neutering, however, **is** a very important consideration. If un-neutered, females will come into heat approximately every six to eight months – which could result in mood swings and aggressiveness towards other females – and there is, of course, the risk of unwanted pregnancy. Both males and females, but males to a greater extent, can adopt unwanted sexual behaviours like lifting their legs inside the house to mark their territory.

Neutering can be the answer to these behaviours in both sexes, and we will look at this in more detail in the chapter 'Going forward'.

One or two?

If you're considering more than one Cockapoo, it's always better to get one at a time. This is so you can get a feel for the crossbreed, as well as the cost and effort required, before taking on a second one. But even if you already have your heart set on two, it's best not to get them from the same litter. That would prevent the puppies from bonding with you rather than with each other and, on top of that, behaviour problems with siblings are common.

Having answers to these questions will help you to narrow your search when you start looking for litters. In all cases, the first thing to find out about is ancestry. Establish which of the three Cocker Spaniels and which of the three Poodles feature in the litter's breeding line, and try to ascertain the ratio too. If nothing else, a basic understanding of the mix will help you to get a sense of the puppies' size and exercise needs. If you'd prefer a small dog with minimal bounce, for example, you don't want to be looking at a litter from a Standard Poodle and a working Cocker Spaniel.

TIMING

The best time to pick up your puppy

As well as getting a rough idea of the sort of Cockapoo you're looking for, you need to decide on the best time to bring your puppy home. This should be at the beginning of a stretch when you, or most of the family, will be home and able to care for her full-time for most of the day. If you're retired this mightn't be a consideration, but if you're a working family with school-going children, for example, you should try to pick your puppy up early in the school holidays.

The weather is another consideration. If you live in a country or area where the summer and winter temperatures are very different, or the wet seasons are extreme, then getting your puppy at the start of a warm or dry season will make for easier toilet training.

Luckily, any breeders in your area are likely to have taken these facts into consideration, so these will be the times when most puppies are available.

A Cockapoo puppy, or a puppy of any breed for that matter, should never leave its mother and the litter before eight weeks. And if the litter is bred from a Toy Poodle, this should be closer to ten weeks. This is a crucial development stage when puppies are building their immune systems and learning important lessons from their mother and litter mates. So once you've decided when it will be most convenient to bring a new puppy home, work back these weeks to figure out ideally when your prospective puppy will be, or will have been, born. Ideally you'll want to visit the puppies around the six-week mark.

When to start looking

Many breeders advertise litters as soon as the mother is pregnant, so it's wise not to leave your search to the last few weeks. If you're looking for a family pet, your search shouldn't take more than a few months. However, if you're looking for a dog that is breeding- or assistance-dog quality you could be looking for up to two years before actually bringing your puppy home. You might be in contact with a breeder before the litter is born, or even before the mother is mated.

But no matter when you start your search, it should begin with identifying the most responsible route to finding puppies for sale in your area.

THE BREEDER

Those first crucial weeks

Choosing the right breeder is one of the most important decisions you will make in choosing your puppy.

The breeder is not only the person who's made the important breeding decisions, he or she is also the person your puppy will spend the crucial first weeks of her life with. I cannot overestimate the significance of the role this person plays in shaping the temperament, character and even behaviour of your puppy.

The next chapter, 'Buying Responsibly' is arguably the most important in this book.

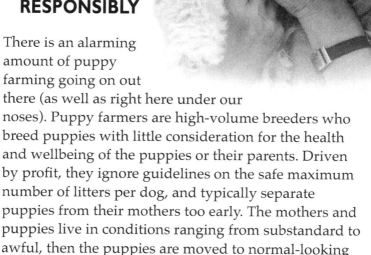

4. BUYING RESPONSIBLY

There is an alarming amount of puppy farming going on out there (as well as right here under our noses). Puppy farmers are high-volume breeders who breed puppies with little consideration for the health and wellbeing of the puppies or their parents. Driven by profit, they ignore guidelines on the safe maximum number of litters per dog, and typically separate puppies from their mothers too early. The mothers and puppies live in conditions ranging from substandard to awful, then the puppies are moved to normal-looking homes for viewings – homes which are, in reality, nothing more than a shop front.

So when arranging to see a litter, make sure it's with a responsible breeder. You want to be certain you are buying a healthy, happy puppy and, at the same time, not unknowingly supporting the cruel puppy trade.

Online adverts might seem like the obvious place to start your search, but good breeders are likely to belong to a Cockapoo club or organisation, so it would be far better to start there (see 'Useful Contacts' at the end of the book). Other good people to ask are vets, dog trainers and behaviour experts in your area. Try to keep your search local because you want to find breeders close enough to your home for you to be able to visit the litter at least once, and be able to pick up your puppy in person.

First contact

Now to make the call. Emailing is your next best option but you will learn so much more by speaking to the breeder in person. These are some key questions to ask:

- Did you breed the puppies yourself?
    It's imperative they did so you can meet the mother.
- What can you tell me about their ancestry?
    Find out which of the three types of Cocker Spaniels and Poodles feature in the breeding. Find out about the parents' and grandparents' temperaments, coat types and colouring. And ask about the F numbers or generation of the puppies. If they make light of these questions, you should stay away.
- How many puppies are, or were there, in the litter?
    This is to avoid seeing just one puppy. You want to make sure you see all the puppies together so you can compare them and see how they interact.
- If I visit, will I see all the puppies together with their mother and in the place where they were bred?
    This must be a 'yes' and that is where you need to meet the mother as well as the litter.
- For how long have you bred Cockapoos, and is it only Cockapoos that you breed?
    They might also breed pure Cocker Spaniels or Poodles for example, but ideally no more than that because multi-breed breeders are more likely to be backyard breeders or puppy farmers.

- Are you a member of any breed clubs?

    You might've already checked, but if not, ideally this should be a 'yes'. And be sure to check their answers for yourself after the call.

- How old is the mother? And is this her first litter?

    She should be over 18 months old, and no more than eight. She should have had no more than four litters in her lifetime, and no more than one litter in the space of a year.

- What will happen to the mother when you've finished breeding with her?

    Ideally she will stay part of her already-loving home.

- Have the puppies or their mother had any health problems?

- What health screening has been done for both parents?

    You want to know if there are any hereditary health problems that could affect the puppies going forward. There is more on this in the next section, 'The paperwork'. If the breeder doesn't believe in health testing, stay away.

- At what age do you recommend your puppies leave you for their new homes?

    This should never be before eight weeks.

- How many people interact with the puppies on a daily basis?

    Ideally you want the puppies to be experiencing the comings and goings of a family household.

- Will they have been treated for worms before they leave for their new homes?

    They should have had at least one deworming treatment by then.

- Will they have been given their first vaccinations?
  Vaccination requirements vary from country to country, but initial vaccinations generally comprise two doses with an interval of two to four weeks. The first of these is usually given around eight weeks.
- Will they have they been microchipped?
  This is a tiny chip injected under your puppy's skin at the back of his neck. It holds his unique number which links to your contact details and, unlike a collar and tag, it stays there for life. In the UK it is law for all puppies to have been microchipped by eight weeks of age.
- Do you have the relevant paperwork?
  The breeder must be able to give you a record of any vaccinations as this will need to be seen by the vet, as well as taken to any training classes or boarding kennels. They must also give you the relevant details if your puppy has been microchipped so you can change the contact details to your own. If there are health screening results for the parents, you should be able to see these too.

There are a lot of questions to be asked, and you don't want this to come across like an interrogation, but you are taking on a new family member who will hopefully be with you for the next 12-15 years. You will be spending a lot of money, and possibly travelling a long distance. These questions needn't all be answered in the first call, but they **are** legitimate, and a good breeder will be understanding – appreciative even.

A good and responsible breeder:
- will be happy to answer all your questions on the phone.

- will ask questions of you too, to make sure their puppies are going to excellent homes.
- will have photos and possibly video clips of the puppies' parents, and be happy to send you more by phone or email if you feel you need them (especially if a visit means a lengthy journey on your part).
- will give you the impression of actively loving and nurturing each pup, as well as the mother, to make sure they are well socialised.
- will be happy to arrange a time for you to visit the puppies and their mother in the place where they were born and raised.
- will be happy for you to have more than one visit before pick-up if you feel you need it.
- might give you references of people who've bought puppies from them in the past.
- might give you some form of guarantee against genetic illnesses.
- might offer to take the dog back if you can't keep it. Some breeders even include a contract requiring you to contact them first if you should ever need to give it up.

A responsible breeder will NEVER:
- offer to deliver the puppy to you.
- offer to meet you at a random place.
- tell you the mother is out at the vets, or for any other reason. If she isn't there, the puppy most likely wasn't bred there, or there could be a problem with the mother.
- set up the visit so you will see just one puppy. (You should always see the puppies together.)

- tell you the litter has been vaccinated before four weeks of age.
- advise you to take a puppy before at least eight weeks of age.
- suggest that you breed your puppy for money.
- push you for payment.

Adverts

If you have had no luck finding a litter through breed clubs and dog experts, then you could have a look what's advertised on more general websites, but be wary. These are some early puppy-farmer warning signs.

- They often use the same contact number on more than one advert. If the advert is posted on the internet, do a search on the number see if it has been used on any other puppy adverts.
- They often use the same descriptions, word-for-word, in more than one advert. Search a key phrase in the wording to locate duplicate advertising.
- Photos of the puppies or the parents may also have been used on other adverts.

Price

Don't look for a bargain – responsibly bred Cockapoos aren't cheap. But be just as wary of puppies priced over the average, because silly money can never guarantee you a perfect dog. Don't be fooled by promises of 'free puppy packs' either – they don't necessarily make the seller any more legitimate.

NEVER get a puppy if you have any doubts about the seller or breeder.

Once you've found a breeder you are sure is responsible and caring, and you've identified a litter of puppies you like the look and sound of, and you're as sure as you can be that they're healthy, happy and from a good home environment, set up your visit or visits.

Then find or buy a soft, comfortable cloth or small blanket to take with you. This is so that, if you **do** reserve a puppy, you can leave it with him until you pick him up. It will absorb the smells of his mother and the litter mates until then, and help to make the separation less stressful.

TIP
Let this comfy blanket absorb the smells of you,
your house and your family before you go. Put it in
the dirty laundry basket for a few hours. That should
do the trick!

Then the countdown begins ...

… well almost.

5. THE PAPERWORK

First there's the
inevitable
paperwork to
consider.

All paperwork can be subject to faking; nothing can guarantee how your dog will turn out; and anyway there's no reason your adorable Cockapoo shouldn't be a wonderful and healthy companion without any paperwork at all. But checking the paperwork is an excellent way to minimise the risk.

If it can be sent electronically, aim to see as much of it as you can before the first visit. In summary, this is what the breeder needs to have shown or given you before you take your puppy home:

1. Health certifications and ratings (for the parents)
2. Vaccination and deworming records
3. Microchipping details
4. Pedigree documents (if the puppies are F1)
5. Health guarantees (if applicable)
6. Sales contract

1. Health certifications and ratings

Genetic diseases can be passed to crossbreeds as well as pure breeds, so even though a Cockapoo, and especially an F1, is usually a healthy dog, it's still important to check health-clearance certificates and ratings for both of the litter's parents.

Essential tests:

- **Annual eye screening** – all Cockapoos registered with the Cockapoo Club of Great Britain must show 'clear' results for prcd-PRA (progressive rod-cone degeneration-Progressive Retinal Atrophy). In the US, eye testing should have been conducted by a DACVO-qualified eye specialist.

Recommended tests:

- **Hip evaluation** – parent dogs (more importantly on the Poodle side) will ideally have been hip-scored for hip dysplasia by the BVA in the UK or OFA in the US. The lower the score the better, but you want it no higher than 13.
- **FN (an inherited kidney disease)** – testing is advisable if there is English Cocker Spaniel in the bloodline. At least one parent's result must be 'clear'.
- **Luxating patellar (loose kneecaps)** – vet-approved evaluation of the knee and stifle joints is also advised.

2. Vaccination and deworming records

You will need your puppy's own paperwork here. This is to take to your vet as well as to any training classes she might attend or kennels she might need to board at.

3. Microchipping details

If the puppies have been microchipped, you will need your puppy's individual number and the name of the provider so you can change the existing contact details to your own.

4. Pedigree certificates (for F1 puppies)

These show your dog's family tree and list the breeding decisions that have been made. For F1 puppies these should be provided from both parents.

5. Health guarantees (if applicable)

Some responsible breeders will also supply a guarantee with their pups that covers them against certain health problems.

6. Sales contract

You might also want to see the sales contract that will need to be signed by both parties on pick-up.

6. WHICH PUPPY?

On the day of your visit you'll be itching to get going, but before you set off, remember to take that soft blanket to leave with the puppies in case you do decide to take one of them.

When you arrive, you'll be magnetically drawn to the litter and all well-grounded, sensible thinking will start to disintegrate, but try not to let down your instantly-falling-in-love guard. Not right away.

Basic checks

First try to make sense of the puppies' environment. Is it warm, friendly and homely? You want to be as sure as you can be that this is where they've grown up. Watch how the breeder interacts with the puppies too. Ideally they are being bought up right underfoot and getting lots of human contact. And if you were promised any paperwork, ask to see it.

The mother

Spend some time with the puppies' mother. She **must** be friendly and good-natured if that is what you hope for in your puppy. You should also consider whether she is the actual mother because sadly this does need checking. Does she look like she's just had the litter? And does she interact with her little ones?

The puppies

FINALLY. You can immerse yourself in the writhing bundle of fluffy heart-melters. But keep your wits about you. Study their temperaments and make sure they are:

- happy and confident,
- friendly and interactive,
- and interested in you and everything around them.

And make sure they look healthy?

- They should appear well-fed, but not pot-bellied.
- Their coats should be clean and soft, with no bald patches, fleas or ticks.
- Their noses should be clean, cool and damp, and their breathing should be quiet.
- Their eyes should be clear and bright, with no sign of discharge, and they should not be blinking a lot.
- The ears should be clean and not smelly.
- Their gums should be a healthy pink or black in colour.
- There should be no irritation around the genitals or bottom, or signs of diarrhoea.
- They should walk and run with no difficulty.

Which puppy?

All still going well, you can start choosing. But which one? There are no right or wrong puppies, just ones that are more or less suited to you, your family and your other pets. For example, if you already have a dominant dog, a submissive puppy would be a sensible choice. Here are some tips that could help you with your decision:

- Don't rush this. Sit down with the puppies and spend all the time you need with them.

- If you are absolutely sure you want a boy, you could ask the breeder to remove the girls while you meet the boys, or vice versa.

- Play with each one to see how they interact with you. If you play with one then turn away, does it follow you? If not, it is likely to be more independent than a puppy that does.

- Distance yourself and study their energy levels. Some will be more active than others and need more exercise. If you want to walk out lots and play games, choose the busy puppy, and if you lead a quiet life and want cuddles, choose one with a laid-back personality.

- Watch how they interact with their litter mates. This could be an indication of how easy they will be to socialise. For example, if another puppy yelps, do they stop playing quite so roughly? If they play nicely they are more likely to grow into adult dogs that play well with other dogs.

- Sort out which are more dominant and which more submissive. The more dominant puppies will take food and toys from the others, and only seem really happy when they are on top of the pile while play fighting. More submissive puppies will play happily with their litter mates without trying to dominate. They will allow other dogs to win a toy, or back off when other puppies want the food or a toy. Some puppies are neither, and prefer being on their own.

- Tell the breeder about your family and any other pets, and ask them for their opinion, because they should have experience with the breed and will also have had time to get to know the individual pups.

- Make a noise behind the puppies. Clap your hands for example. If they flinch, that might be a sign of a nervous disposition, and if they don't react, it could be an indication of poor hearing.
- Throw something to see if they run after it, or bring it back.
- As a test, try placing the puppies on their backs and gently resting your fingers on their chests. The puppies that struggle to get free are less patient than the ones that make little effort to get away. You can also do this test by gently lifting the puppies off the floor, just a foot and for a few seconds, keeping them horizontal.

A good choice is an even-tempered puppy with an outgoing nature. But it's often said that you don't choose your dog or puppy, it chooses you, and many people vouch for this. One puppy might spend your entire visit convincing you he's the one you want to take home, and if that's the case, he probably is.

Whichever pup you choose, when you've settled on your choice, that will be the best dog in the world, and time after time you will ask yourself how you got to be **so** lucky.

Before you leave

(assuming you're coming back for the puppy at a later date)

Identity – If your chosen puppy looks like any of the others, make sure you and the breeder can tell which is yours. For example, the owner might put a coloured collar on your puppy.

Deposit – The breeder will most likely ask for a deposit to secure your puppy. Make sure you get a receipt and a written agreement that the contract is only binding if the puppy is in good health when you collect it.

Sales contract – Confirm with the breeder that they will have a puppy contract ready at the time of collection. This should include details of health screening (for the puppy and its parents); details of the parents; all information to date on vaccinations, deworming, microchipping and veterinary visits; and a health guarantee (if applicable).

Food and care – Find out whatever you can about meals. What are the puppies being fed at the moment? How much and how often? Ask to see the food so you can be sure of giving him exactly what he is used to when you bring him home.

Finally, ask the breeder if you can leave your soft puppy blanket with the litter so that when you pick him up, you'll be able to bring all those familiar mummy-puppy smells with him into his new home.

7. PREPARING FOR THE BIG DAY

It almost goes without saying that when you pick up your bundle of joy, and destruction too, you will need buckets of love, oodles of patience and a fantastic sense of humour. But you will also need to do a surprising amount of planning, puppy-proofing and purchasing of paraphernalia …

Things to do
- Arrange a date to pick up your puppy when it has passed the eight-week mark. If you will be travelling by car, it should be a day when at least one other person can accompany the driver.
- Book a visit to the vet for about two days after pick up.
- If you will be taking out pet insurance, do your homework now so you can have it in place as soon as you bring your puppy home.
- Puppy proof your home, checking every nook and cranny:
  - Secure the property. This is the most important thing you can do to keep your puppy safe. If you have a garden or yard, ensure the wall or fence is escape proof from the ground up.
  - If there is a pool, pond or any deep water she could fall into, fence it off.
  - Check that there are no chemicals within reach –

pesticides (including slug pellets), weedkillers, fertilisers, etc.

- Consider fitting child locks to bins and low cupboards that might contain these or other potentially dangerous items.
- Cover or hide electricity cables and wires.
- Tie up, secure or pack away anything that could topple over or be pulled by a cord or cable, like a kettle or a heavy bookcase.
- Remove sharp objects and small things she could choke on.
- Be aware of any plants in your house and garden that may be poisonous. It's worth checking online for a comprehensive list, but these are some of the more common varieties: Aloe Vera, Asparagus Fern, Azalea, Castor Bean, Corn Cockle, Crocus, Cyclamen, Daffodil, Holly Berry, Foxglove, Ivy (Hedera Helix), Jade (Crassula Ovata), Jerusalem Cherry, Jessamine, Hyacinth, Lily of the Valley, Milkweed, Mistletoe, Oleander, Philodendron,

Rhododendron, Sweet Pea, Tulip, Water Hemlock, Wisteria.
- ◦ Also be aware of low lying plants with sharp pointed leaves.
- ◦ Remove valuables from the floor.

- Decide on her special place, a suitable comfy space that she can make her own. This is where her crate will be positioned if you choose to use one, or her play pen, or simply her basket and toys. This special place should be somewhere central – somewhere that she can feel safe, but without feeling isolated or excluded. An ideal position would be against a wall in the room that most of you spend the most time in during the day. If you already have another dog, it should be away from your other dog's special place, at least for starters.

Things to buy, make or borrow
- **Soft blanket** – if you left this with the litter when you chose your puppy, be sure to collect it when you pick her up. Those familiar smells will help makes the transition far less stressful.
- **A crate** (also commonly referred to as a cage or den) – this is optional of course, but it would serve as your puppy's own space, a special place where she can be safe, quiet and keep her toys. There is more about this in the next three chapters, but for now choose one that is just big enough for your puppy's basket or bed, a couple of toys and her bowls. Wire cages are better ventilated than plastic ones, offer better views, and are easily collapsible.
- **Comfortable dog bed** – this could be a basket, a dog cushion or even a folded blanket, as long as it's soft, comfortable and easily washable.

- **A harness** – this is to prevents unnecessary pressure on her throat when she is learning to walk on the lead. It should be a suitable size, adjustable, and comfortable.
- **A collar** – choose one that is soft, lightweight and comfortable. She will soon outgrow it and you can choose a sturdier one then if that's what you prefer.
- **An ID tag** – keep it small and light and have it engraved with her name and your contact details.
- **Short lead** (four to six foot long) – again, nice and light. She's only little.
- **Extendable lead** – these can be dangerous and are not always permitted in parks and conservation areas. That said, used carefully and only once your puppy is used to the short lead, an extendable lead can make walks more enjoyable for you and your puppy.
- **A puppy coat** – if you live in a cold climate.
- **Bowls** – go for a non-tip, non-slip design. You might also consider a non-spill travel bowl for car trips, and a crate bowl that clips onto the door or side of your puppy's crate so that it can't be overturned. Remember your puppy could be a medium-sized adult dog before long, so consider whether to invest in medium-sized bowls now, or get small bowls for now and upsize in time.
- **Food** – start with the diet your puppy has been on at her breeders. After that you can move her on to the food of your choice. If you are concerned about making the best decision, consult your vet at her first check-up.
- **Treats** – you will need lots of these. They are fantastic motivators when your puppy is first

learning the rules, and excellent for reinforcing good behaviour. They should be suitable for puppies and healthy (avoid additives and preservatives, as well as rawhide treats which could get stuck in her throat).

- **A treat pouch** – a handy pocket for loose treats that keeps your own pockets from constantly smelling of dog food. Another option is a small sealable tub that you can shake the treats in noisily to get her attention.
- **Chews** – your puppy will spend around four hours of each day munching on things, so it's up to you to provide what you want her to do this munching on. Chews are essentially long-lasting treats, and make a fabulous alternative to table legs and leather shoes, but with a young puppy avoid any chews that can splinter. Antler horns are good, and so are Kong toys filled with treats.
- **Toys** – can a puppy have too many toys? I think not. Invest in plenty of toys in all shapes, sizes, textures, colours and smells. She will chew on them, play with them and even snuggle up with them for hours. (It's wise to avoid giving her old shoes because, smart as she is, she's unlikely to differentiate between old and new when she slips inside your shoe closet.)
- **Anti-chew or citronella** – it's worth investing in either of these to spray onto those things she absolutely must not chew on. Expensive chair legs for example.
- **Poo(p) bags** – biodegradable
- **Newspaper** – or equivalent wee-mat material for house-training

- **Carpet cleaner and odour eliminator** – buy these separately or as one product, but make sure it says 'pet friendly'.
- **Hot water bottle** – strong and well covered
- **Grooming kit** – a soft brush or a grooming glove, and a dog shampoo. Don't cheat and use a shampoo for human hair. In time you are also likely to need another brush or comb, blunt-nosed hair scissors, electric clippers and a pair of dog nail clippers, and you might decide on a dog dental-care kit too, but there's no need for any of those right now.
- **Dog gates/baby gates/stair gates** – these are far better than closed doors for keeping a room off-limits. There's a huge choice on the market, but stay away from stretch gates that she could get her head stuck in.
- **Play pen** – this is useful if you are leaving her for a couple of hours because it is big enough for her to sleep, play and poop in if necessary.
- **Car seat, pet travel carrier or dog guard** – if she is likely to be driven around you will need a safe form of restraint. There is more on this in the chapter 'Travelling by car'.

Setting the rules

Before you bring your newest family member into your home, it's essential for you and the other existing members of the household to have a serious chat about the rules. Decide among yourselves where your puppy will be allowed, and when. Make sure you are all in agreement about which rooms and pieces of furniture are off-limit. And make sure everyone understands that sneaking her into an off-limit area, or letting her break the rules in any other way, would only be unfair on the puppy in the long run.

If your family agrees that she is not to be allowed on your best chair, it doesn't mean you need to treat her like an underling. You can compromise by making sure she has a place she can call her own – a special bed placed next to the forbidden chair for example.

Choosing a name

You could choose this once your puppy is home, but either way her name is more important than you might think. You will be using it several times a day for years to come so it must be something she will easily recognise.

- Dogs respond better to shorter names – one-syllable names with a hard consonant or consonants like Pip or Zac for example, or two-syllable names like Bu-ddy or Cor-ky. You might love the name Jemima or Octavia, but your puppy would thank you for calling her Jem or Otto instead.
- Make sure the name you choose doesn't sound too much like a commonly used command: No, Sit, Down, Stay, Come, Here, Good or Fetch. Beau and Jo, for example, sound too much like No.
- And don't choose a name that sounds like that of another member of the household. If your mother is called Anne, don't call puppy Dan; if your cat is Tigger, don't call puppy Digger or Trigger.
- Never give any dog a name you wouldn't be happy calling out loud in public

8. PICKING UP YOUR PUPPY

The big day has finally arrived. If possible, pick your puppy up early in the day so he can spend lots of time in his new environment before facing his first night without his mother and litter mates.

If you are driving, try to take someone with you to comfort him, but don't take too many people because the journey should be calm and quiet.

Before you go

- If you haven't already set up his special place in a safe but central spot, do that now. Crate or no crate, furnish it with the comfortable dog basket or bed, some toys, and also some treats if you like.
- And if you haven't already sprayed your most valued furniture with anti-chew, now's a very good time.

Things to take

- The remainder of the payment (if necessary)
- An absorbent mat (or similar protection) in case he relieves himself in the car
- Poo bags and cleaning cloths
- Two bowls (one for food and one for water)
- A small amount of food (in a container)
- A bottle of water
- A small selection of toys and chews

- A backup soft blanket or cushion is also a good idea (in case something has happened to the one you left with the breeder)
- A collar or harness and your lead (not extendable)
- A travel crate (if that's your preference) with an item of clothing inside that smells of you.

The big moment

You'll be a bundle of emotions when you arrive – ridiculously excited, slightly nervous and everything in between. That's understandable. This is a big moment! Life is about to change for you, and the world as he knows it is about to change for your puppy. Give him a gentle but gargantuan cuddle, have a play and check that he's still in good health:

- happy, confident and curious,
- that there are no signs of mucus from the nose, bottom or genitals,
- and that his ears are clean and not smelly.

In the excitement

Apart from your new and perfect puppy, don't forget to come away with:

- the blanket you left, if you left one
- the relevant paperwork including:
  - a receipt of payment
  - health records detailing check-ups and procedures, including the vaccination certificate
  - microchip details if relevant (so you can register the puppy under your name).

It's also worth double checking his food type (just in case it's changed), and finding out what times he has been having his meals.

And last but definitely not least, remember to thank the mother and the breeder for your beautiful puppy.

Travelling

Make sure your puppy's feeling safe and happy to be with you before you take him away for good. He is totally reliant on you now, so put yourself into those little paws that are being taken away from their mother and litter mates. Realise that he is leaving the only place he has ever known and, if you're driving, getting into a car for the first time too! Ask yourself, "How would I be feeling now?" and "What would I need from this new person or family?" You'd want to feel safe and secure, loved and cherished.

Put his collar or harness on before you set off. This is best done with two people so one of you can hold and distract him while the other puts it on. You don't want it too tight or too loose. You should just be able to put two fingers under the collar, or two fingers between your puppy and the harness at any point.

If you're travelling by car, your puppy would be happiest being held by the passenger in the back seat. He would need to be held securely (legally speaking 'suitably restrained'), so that the driver is not distracted, and be given love and constant reassurance on the journey. However, where you put him in the car will depend on the laws in your country or state, because holding him in the back seat could affect your insurance.

If you've brought a travel crate instead, then arrange the comfy blanket inside, with its scents of mum and the litter mates, as well as the item of clothing that smells of you. Place him gently inside and fasten the seatbelt over the crate. The passenger should sit next to the crate to comfort him. He will probably be too anxious for toys, but offer them anyway.

If the journey home is a long one, you'll need to stop every hour – more if you can. Offer him some of the food and water in the bowls you've brought along, and give him a little walk and the chance to go to the toilet. But always keep him on the lead. Though he's unlikely to stray from you, this would be a terrible place for him to get loose.

Like people, dogs can suffer from travel sickness, so it is possible he might be feeling a little ill or even be sick on the journey.

9. THE HOMECOMING

If you don't already have another dog or other dogs, you might want to skip to the end of this next list of bullet points. But if you do, here are some tips on how to introduce them safely and sensibly.

- Stay outside while you introduce them.
    - If possible, arrange for them to meet for the first time away from home. Ideally, choose somewhere your older dog hasn't been before so that the excitement of the new environment will

dilute the puppy's presence. Your puppy is unlikely to be protected by her vaccinations at this stage, so try to choose somewhere no other dogs are likely to go.

- If they do need to meet at home, however, let them meet outside before taking your puppy in.
- Whether they meet at home or away, keep introductions short and sweet to start with, with both dogs on a lead.
- Stand still or walk slowly while they get acquainted, and try not to interfere.
- At home, take your puppy into the house first, before letting the older dog in.
- Lift any pre-existing dog toys and food bowls off the floor for a few days.
- If you already have two other dogs or more, the process is the same but it's imperative that you introduce the puppy to just one at a time.

Whether or not there are other dogs, give her a chance to wee before going inside. Then, when you're ready, carry her into the house and put her in the special place you've created for her, or in her crate (with the door open wide). Sit beside her, arrange the blanket smelling of her mother and litter mates in her basket, and give her a treat.

When she's explored her special place, let her venture into all the areas of the house she will be allowed in, so that she knows this is home. If there are areas of the house that will be off limits to her, then it is better not to let her in there from the start than to change the rules at some later stage. She will be feeling overwhelmed, nervous even, so stay close by her side, a reassuring presence.

All the treats today should be given in her crate or special area – her very own bedroom. Her comfy blanket should stay there and it's advisable to feed her there too. Do everything you can think of to make her feel that this is the best and safest place in the world. If she has a crate and the design is very open, cover it with a blanket leaving gaps she can see out of.

Puppies wee about once an hour and poop several times a day, so take her to a suitable toilet place every hour if you can. She will still piddle and poop wherever and whenever she needs to because she is so little, can't talk to you, and has no idea that in some places this is a no-no. Toilet training is covered in more detail later on, but for now be sure to clean up very well, always using an odour eliminator.

Your puppy needs 18-22 hours' sleep a day at this age, and on this momentous day she is bound to need even more, so try not to overload her senses with too many people or too much excitement. But **your** presence is essential for her peace of mind so, when you're sitting quietly, let her sit with you and sleep on your lap or close by. If your family has agreed that she is not to be allowed on the furniture, then sit on the floor with her in these early days.

Make sure there is always fresh water available to her, and that she knows where it is. Feed her what she is used to and, as far as practical, at the times she is used to. (This is probably three or four evenly-spaced meals a day.) She might not want to eat at first and that's okay, she'll eat when she's ready. Take the food away and re-present it to her a little later.

Aim to give her her last meal of the day a good two hours before her bedtime, so she has a chance to go to the toilet before settling down for her first night.

10. NEW PUPPY SAFETY

Now that your puppy's home, the best way to keep him safe is through your and your family's or housemates' own diligence.

- Handle him gently and carry him carefully.
- Keep doors and gates closed and open where necessary.
- Don't shut doors too quickly – your new 'shadow' could be right on your heels.
- Make a habit of looking where you're walking too. He might've been sleeping in the next room just two seconds ago, but that's no reason to assume he's still there now.
- Don't let him play around cars, or even the lawn mower.
- Don't let him near the edges of pools or deep water.
- Be careful with heights too. Don't let him near high balconies, low window ledges, or unsecured staircases.
- Keep electrical cords well out of reach. Apart from shock there is the danger of pulling something down on top of himself (a heavy iron or a boiling kettle).
- Be extra careful with moving or folding furniture such as rocking chairs, recliners and retractable baby or stair gates.

Small children

If you have small children, they must be taught NOW that he is not a toy.

- They must not be allowed to pick him up without adult supervision.
- They must not be allowed to disturb him if he is sleeping or has taken himself to a quiet place.
- They must leave him alone while he is eating. Meal times should be uninterrupted so there is no need for him to gulp down his food.
- Games should be calm, and if your puppy gets over-excited they should keep still rather than running around squealing.

Other dogs

- If you're worried about your puppy's safety with any existing dogs, use a baby gate or stair gate to separate them in the short term, or put the puppy in his crate or a play pen while the dogs get used to each other.
- Make sure all members of the family give the older dog more attention than usual.
- Feed your puppy in his special place for now. Even later, when your dogs are fed together, their eating places should be at least six feet apart.

Cats

When your puppy is this young, he is unlikely to be a problem for your cat. Cockapoos generally get on well with the family cat, especially if they have grown up with it. But to be on the safe side introduce them with care and be ready for some lively interaction.

- Keep your puppy on a lead when they first meet, and have a lovely treat ready. If your cat responds by hissing to begin with, your puppy will most likely retreat. But if the cat runs away, be ready to distract the puppy with the treat so he doesn't chase after it.

- If the introduction becomes unpleasant, separate them and try again later. They could be at odds for several weeks until they reach an agreement.
- Always restrain your puppy around the cat until he learns that the cat is not something to be chased.
- Distract him with a toy to teach him that playing with people is more fun than chasing the cat. It's debatable, but that's what we want him to think.
- Don't leave them alone together until you know they can get along.
- If you need to keep your puppy and the cat apart while you're out, use the crate, pen or a stair gate.
- Make sure the cat has safe places high up that it can reach instead of having to run away.

CURIOUS THINGS

Your puppy will be chewing on everything now, using his mouth to find out about the world around him But there are some 'curiosities' it's particularly important to keep out of his reach:

Non-edibles
- Medication – human medication is the biggest cause of pet poisoning
- Human vitamin supplements
- Anti-freeze and other chemicals – many of these are sweet-tasting
- Paint thinner
- Pesticides, weedkillers and fertilisers

- Toothpaste
- Sponges
- Household cleaners (including toilet cleaners)
- A surprisingly high number of household and garden plants can be poisonous when eaten in large amounts. (See the shortlist and advice in 'Preparing for the big day'.)
- Small metal objects like coins, and nuts and bolts
- Pins, needles and other sharp objects, including spiky low-lying plants.

People food

It's always best to feed your puppy or dog actual puppy or dog food, and simply stay clear of treats from your own plate. But there are some people foods that you must never let him get hold of never mind feed him because, while they are perfectly safe for human consumption, they are poisonous and potentially fatal to dogs. These include:

- Chocolate (especially dark chocolate)
- Xylitol (an artificial sweetener, commonly used in sweets and gum, but also in some sweet foods like low-calorie cake)
- Alcohol
- Onion
- Garlic
- Grapes or raisins
- Avocado.

Also keep dogs away from

- Soft or cooked bones (especially from chicken or pork, as they could get stuck in his throat)
- Macadamia nuts

- Fruit pips or seeds
- Potato peels or green potatoes
- Rhubarb leaves
- Baker's yeast or yeast dough
- Caffeine
- Mushrooms
- Hops (generally in beer).

Dog products

And don't assume everything at a pet shop will be puppy-friendly. Avoid:

- Cow hooves which can splinter
- Raw hide and pigs' ears which can be a choking hazard
- Toys that might become stringy when chewed
- Chew toys made of plastic or soft rubber
- Toys with small parts they could choke on.

Call the vet immediately if you suspect your puppy has eaten something potentially harmful.

Put yourself in your puppy's paws

If you want to be really proactive, put yourself in his itchy paws and busy jaws for just a moment. Being careful not to underestimate his size, determination or intelligence, get down on all fours and examine every nook and cranny to see what temptations call. Then take these away. Get everything out of his reach. Make it as difficult as you can for him to get into any form of danger or trouble.

Then watch over him, just as you would a busy toddler.

11. THE FIRST NIGHT

Crunch time! She's had her supper, a couple of hours ago, and it's time for bed.

Take her outside for a last chance to go to the toilet. Stay with her in the place you'd most like her to go, and be patient. If she goes, make a big fuss of her.

Back inside, make sure her crate or safe space is as appealing as possible, with her comfortable bed and her soft blanket. In the short term, some people make this space in their own bedrooms, setting it up by the side of their beds. Considering the trauma of this first night, to your puppy and yourselves, there is a lot to be said for this. She still wouldn't be able to snuggle up the way she's used to, but at least she could see you and hear you and would know she's not alone.

If her sleeping place is a metal crate, the openness still leaves your puppy quite exposed. So if you've chosen the crate option and haven't already done so, put a blanket over it, making sure she can always see out.

It's a good idea to make a warm, but not too warm, hot water bottle, and wrap it carefully into her comfy blanket. This is to replicate the body warmth of her mother and litter mates when they're snuggled up. You could also put a ticking clock in the bed to mimic a heartbeat. (Another option is comforter toy – they offer warmth and a pulsing 'heartbeat', but they're not cheap.) And if the special place is not in your room, consider leaving a radio playing softly to give her the sense she is not alone.

Scatter some toys and treats and make sure she has access to clean water in her non-tip or clip-on bowl.

If the space is big enough to include a place to relieve herself – aside from the bedding and bowls, then cover this with newspaper or an absorbent wee mat.

When crunch time comes, don't fuss over her. Just put her in her crate or special place with a treat, as though she's the luckiest puppy in the world, and close the door: be it a cage door, room door or baby gate.

In all likelihood she will cry at first, but resist the urge to pick her up. If that's where you want her at night, she must learn to stay there from day one. In fact, it's far kinder not to give her any attention when she cries, because any time you 'give in' would just encourage her to cry even harder each time you had to step away again. Be strong for her sake. Know that she is warm, comfortable, fed and tired, and that the cries will soon subside. What's more, she will soon come to like the quiet and safety of her own space.

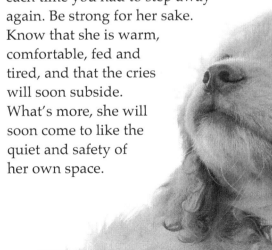

Your bed or hers?

Where your puppy sleeps is up to you of course – there are plenty of arguments both for and against your bed and we will look at a few of these in the chapter on 'Behaviour' – but here are some reasons why her crate or special area is a good idea, at least to start off with.

- She's not yet potty trained, and accidents in your bed are a great deal more difficult to clean up than accidents in her special place.
- There is the risk of her falling off the bed and getting a fright or even an injury.
- When she is this tiny, there is, albeit small, the danger of rolling onto her during the night.
- Once a dog starts sleeping on your bed, it can be a very difficult habit to break.
- If she is allowed to sleep on your bed now, she's more likely to have separation issues later on.

What about night-time toilet times?

If your puppy is in your bedroom and you hear her shuffling around in the night, get up straight away and take her outside and to the place you'd most like her to go. She'll want to avoid messing in her sleeping place if she can help it.

If she's not in your room, you'll need to set an alarm for the middle of the night so you can get up and take her out. Alternatively, and only if you've laid down a wee mat, you could wait until very early the next morning.

At some stage she won't need this break at all, but whichever option you choose, you'll need to keep this up for the next few weeks at least.

12. THE FIRST WEEK

From just three weeks old your puppy has been socialising and learning to play with his mother and litter mates. Now suddenly he must learn to be with you, and with people, and to figure out a whole new set of rules. He is likely to follow you everywhere. Don't be surprised if he seems nervous, whines, cries, or doesn't want to eat. Give him love and constant reassurance. If he shivers, make him warm and hold him close.

Luckily for you he is at his most impressionable during these early days, so the time and effort you put in now to building a positive relationship will be worth buckets of good behaviour over the months and years to come.

Mesmerisingly cute as he is, your gorgeous bundle of innocence also needs to know his position in the household. For his own sense of security, as well as your relationship going forward, he needs to understand straight away that you are the leader.

We will look at discipline and obedience later on but until you've read that far, if he does something you don't want him to do, don't punish him or show aggression in any form. That would only confuse him and make him fearful. Instead:

1. distract him
2. encourage him to do something good instead
3. then reward him for listening.

Encourage and reward – praise him at every opportunity for the good things he does in your eyes, so he can begin to learn what is right in your world.

Be clear and consistent in your praise and he will become the most doting and loyal friend you could ever imagine.

Love him

Unconditionally. Do this and the rest will come naturally.

Teach him his name

Use his name to get his attention, and reward him when he responds to it. But be careful not to say it over and over again or he will quickly become de-sensitised to it.

TIP: Never use his name to scold him. It should encourage him to turn his attention to you.

Handle him

Your puppy needs to learn that he is safe with people, that they mean him no harm, and that he has no reason to fear them or react defensively.

He should start learning this straight away through lots of physical contact. Pet him and handle him: fondle his paws, move his legs, run your hand over his tail, feel his ears, touch his nose, gently examine his teeth, rub his tummy, groom him, bath him. Pick him up and carry him around, supporting him at the chest as well as under his bottom.

Encourage independence

Being so gorgeous you might be tempted to cuddle him and carry him around all the time, but he should also be allowed to explore on his own. With a Cockapoo it's very important to encourage independence.

Keep his special place appealing

Associations with his special place must be positive, so it should NEVER be used for punishment. Make it comfortable and leave toys and treats inside so that it always feels welcoming and homely.

If he has soiled in it, be sure to clean it well.

Encourage him into this space and praise him when he goes in on his own.

Feed and water him

Your puppy should be having three (or maybe four) meals a day at this stage, ideally of the same food he was having with the other puppies in the litter. If you don't know how much to feed him, work out his daily allowance from the instructions on the food packaging. Split this allowance into three or four equal portions and work out a schedule for regular feeding, for example:

- Three feeds: 7am, 12.30pm and 6pm
- Four feeds: 7am, 11am, 3pm and 7pm.

If he's on dry puppy food, you can add a little warm water and let it soak for a minute before feeding him. This makes it easier to eat and digest.

If you have more than one dog, feed them separately – at least six feet apart – to prevent food aggression.

You, or his primary carer if it's not you, should feed him most often. Feed him some of his meal by hand if you like, as this encourages trusting and loyal behaviour going forward.

Water should always be available, and it should be

fresh. Don't cheat by just topping it up. Empty the bowl, scrub it clean and refill it every day.

Make sure the last meal of the day is a good two hours before bedtime so he's less likely to mess in the house during the night.

Manage toilet time

Remember that your puppy needs regular toilet breaks and it's up to you to help him with the when and where.

During the day, take him outside every hour if you can, and lead him to the spot you'd most like him to use. When he does it there, make sure he understands that was a good thing by making a HUGE fuss of him. Give him a treat and tell him what a brilliant, amazing, spectacular dog he is.

At night, he won't want to go to the toilet in his special place but when he is very little he can only hold on for so long, so ideally you should be getting up during the night to take him out, as well as early each morning.

'But what about when he **does** mess inside?' you ask. What of it? He's a baby. Clean up well and be extremely patient. No matter what you've heard or read until now, don't punish him. He won't understand. (There's a whole chapter on toilet training coming up soon.)

Play with him

Spend lots of time playing with him. And encourage him to experience the world through different surfaces. He will be confined to your property until his last vaccinations have taken effect, but you can still introduce him to floor tiles, wood, carpet, grass, sand,

rock, soft cushions, paper and blankets. Let him get used to them all.

Give him quiet time

He needs some time on his own too so he can learn not to be anxious later on when you aren't there or able to play with him. (See 'Time alone' in the next chapter.) Shut him in his special place for a few minutes, once or even twice a day. If you have a garden or back yard, let him outside without you, or just with your other dogs, for ten minutes every now and then.

REMINDER
Never let him get hold of anything listed in the chapter:
'New puppy safety'

Loosen his collar

If he wears a collar, check the fit every few days. He is growing fast and it'll need to be loosened regularly. You should be able to fit two fingers between the collar and his neck.

Visit the vet

Regulations vary from country to country, so my best advice here is to take his vaccination certificate along to the visit and let your vet advise you on what your puppy needs and when. Most vaccines require several rounds, between six weeks and 16 weeks, so scheme these in during this first visit. And be sure to tell the vet if you have plans to take your puppy to puppy classes or boarding kennels, because either of these are likely to require further inoculation.

Get advice on deworming, and the prevention of parasites.

If your puppy has not already been microchipped, you could have that done now. (In the UK, this is a legal requirement.)

If your puppy's baby nails are very long and catching on everything, you could ask the vet or a veterinary nurse to clip them for you, or to show you how to do it yourself.

Make the visit fun for your puppy by giving him praise and attention, staying by his side when he gets his shots, and telling him how good he is. Possibly take him for a walk or give him a treat afterwards to create a positive association.

Take out insurance

If you're planning on taking out pet insurance, but haven't got round to it yet, do that now.

13. EMOTIONAL DEVELOPMENT

FRAGILE! HANDLE WITH CARE

From eight to approximately 12 weeks is the strongest bonding period you will have with your Cockapoo, so it's especially important that you spend it well, giving her lots of time and patience.

She is weaning herself from her mother and you need to be ultra-sensitive to her feelings. Of course, you should always be sensitive to her feelings, but these weeks – known as the 'fear period' – are the very worst time for anything to frighten her. It is a stage when puppies are over-sensitive and when negative stimuli are the most likely to leave a lasting impression. For example, a loud electric storm when your puppy is all alone could lead to a lifelong fear of storms.

But this is also a time of opportunity. It is a particularly good time to show your puppy that most experiences are harmless. And if she's already afraid of something, it's a good time to try to recondition her. For example, if she's afraid of umbrellas, show her that you're not afraid of them by handling them gently in her presence without pressuring her in any way. In fact the more you expose her to the real world now, in a safe and measured way, the more confidence she will have going forward.

SOCIALISATION

In puppy-speak this means introducing her – now while she is still young – to as many people and animals of all shapes, colours and sizes as possible. It is the best way to help your puppy adjust to her new life in your world, and in fact, it is one of the most important things you can do to raise a happy Cockapoo. You will be able to teach her fancy tricks for years to come, but during these next few weeks (her vaccination status permitting) it's vital that you get her out and about. Use the time well and don't let it slip by. Visit friends and have friends to visit her. If puppy parties and puppy training are on offer in your area, take her along. (The chapter 'Stepping out' looks at how to do this safely and considerately.)

If you're struck by the bottom-sniffling that comes with your puppy's meetings and greetings, you'll soon get used to it. It's how dogs say 'hello', suss each other out and even determine whether they've met before.

HABITUATION

This means exposing her – now while she is still young – to as many new places and conditions as possible. In all fairness, you can't shut her indoors then expect her to behave normally in new environments.

As soon as her vaccinations have taken effect, take her with you everywhere you can and let her explore. Let her discover different smells, surfaces, sounds and sights. Take her into a park, to the school gates, for a walk along a river; go to a sports match, go to the shops, paddle through puddles. Walk her over and under bridges. Let her see cars and trucks and trains and planes. Thunder, lightning and snow might be hard to arrange, but ideally let her experience different weather conditions too. Take her out at night and walk her in the rain.

Feeling safe

It is imperative though that during these new experiences she feels safe as well as having fun. Helping her to feel at ease in new situations will go a long way towards helping her grow up to be a happy and well-adjusted dog, so stay close by her side through these new discoveries and don't let any of them frighten or over-excite her. Going forward, she can only be properly receptive to your training when she is feeling confident and secure.

Here are some ideas to help with this.

- If you come across a potentially frightening situation – some big kids playing rough and tumble at the park for example – watch her closely for signs of discomfort. If she's hiding between your legs, or tucking her tail between her legs, you should back off and find a different route.

- Never put her under pressure to get close to anyone or anything.
- Be alert and sensitive to her feelings so you will know when you can approach and when to stay away. There are many signs which mean different things in different contexts. (See the chapter 'Puppy-People Translator').
- If you're not sure how she feels, avoid having a tight lead so she knows she has a choice. If she is curious, approach from a distance. Let her look, listen and smell, gradually closing the distance as she is comfortable.

Accidental noise

Don't forget about background noises that you are accustomed to, but might be frightening for your puppy.

TV, radio and computers – Be alert to sounds from your devices. Dogs barking aggressively, for example, could leave her terrified. Turn the sound down or off if she becomes alarmed – and before then if possible.

Tension in the house – Keep a good vibe in the house. If she hears angry voices or senses a bad mood, she won't understand that it has nothing to do with her (whether it does or not).

Fireworks and thunder – Close doors and windows, and muffle the sound with your own music or voices. Stay close to her, showing her that you're not afraid.

TIME ALONE

Dog owners are increasingly aware of their dogs' need to be socialised and exposed to different experiences, and many go to great lengths to arrange this exposure. But just as many owners forget that being alone is one of these experiences. In fact giving your puppy time alone is helping to equip her with one of her most essential life skills.

Cockapoos are highly social and don't like being alone, but most of them **have** to be at some time or another and the best way to minimise or even prevent separation anxiety at a later stage is to start leaving your puppy on her own now, just occasionally, during the day. If she is lucky enough to be right by your side for most of the time this is even more important. Start practising slowly.

- Choose a time when she is getting tired and likely to sleep soon.
- Take her out for a little play and a toilet break.
- Shut her in her crate or special place with everything she needs.
- Ignore any whining and leave the room or go out for a short while.
- If she is very little and goes to sleep while you are out, open the gate, door or crate door when you return so she can get out when she wakes.
- Start off with about ten minutes and build it up slowly to no more than half an hour at this stage. For one thing, she will soon be needing the toilet.

We will cover this in more depth in the chapter, 'Separation anxiety'.

BARKING

It's especially important not to punish barking during your puppy's first weeks in her new home, for all the reasons we've considered. She should be allowed to explore and to express herself.

If she's barking because she's worried about something, and you know her fear is unfounded, lead her away from it and give her a treat when she is quiet. Reassure her with a gentle voice, then gradually expose her to whatever it is that she is afraid of, showing her that you are with her, that you are not afraid and that there is nothing to worry about.

AGGRESSION

This is unusual in Cockapoos, but don't let that lull you into a false sense of security. Any dog can develop aggressive behaviour. An excellent way to prevent this is by handling your puppy lots and often while she is very young. Teach her now that you can hold and touch her, her toys and her food whenever and however you please. Teach her that you are the leader and you are in charge.

How? By doing just that. Handle her, her toys and her food whenever and however you please. That way she is less likely to become territorial and possessive over what she considers to be her things.

SMALL CHILDREN

Put yourself in your puppy's paws and imagine small children rolling around on the ground with you, giggling and shrieking, and how quickly that would encourage you to mouth and nip. Imagine being picked up continually, carried around, possibly even dropped, pestered, woken up … Think what it would be like not to be able to say, 'I don't want to play any more'.

The only way your puppy knows how to tell someone that she's hurting, tired, frightened or has had enough is to growl or snap. And the best way for you to manage this is to prevent the situation from developing in the first place.

Small children need to learn that your puppy is NOT a toy, and be taught how to behave around her. The following points are reiterated from the chapter 'New puppy safety'.

- They should not be allowed to pick her up without adult supervision.
- They should not be allowed to disturb her if she is sleeping or has taken herself to a quiet place.
- They must leave her alone while she is eating.
- They should not run around squealing, and if the puppy becomes over-excited they should be calm and still.
- They should be allowed to play calm games with the puppy, but nothing involving wrestling or tugging.
- They should stay on their feet while playing, because if they writhe on the ground with the puppy, the puppy is likely to treat them like her litter mates and mouth and bite.

NOTE
Puppies grow up fast compared with human children. One week in your puppy's life is equivalent to around five months' development in a human child.

FURTHER CRATE TRAINING

If you are using a crate and it started off in a temporary position at your bedside overnight, you should move it further from the bedroom – step by step if you like – to its permanent day-time position in the house. But only do this as your puppy grows in confidence and don't rush it. Your job is to build her trust.

If your puppy is going to be in the crate for a lengthy period while you are out, then you should leave her with some food as well as her water and toys, and always keep the area at a comfortable temperature, and free from damp and draughts.

TIPS:
If you want to teach her to like her crate more, try shutting her favourite toy inside for a minute, leaving her on the outside wanting to get in.

Attach a long-lasting chew treat to the inside of the crate – avoiding string she could get tied up in – so that if she wants it, she has to enjoy it right there.

EATING POO – SERIOUSLY?

Your puppy might eat poo – her own or another animal's. But don't panic. Revolting as it is, it's quite common in puppies. It's a difficult issue to address because nobody really knows what it is that makes them do it. The good news is that they pretty much always grow out of it, and quite quickly too.

You might have read or heard advice about upping her vitamin B content, but **never** give her human vitamins. Honestly, apart from sitting it out, the best things you can do are:

- ensure that her diet is nutritionally complete
- clean up as soon as she's pooped
- keep her stocked up with interesting chew toys so she doesn't get bored
- keep her on a leash on walks so you can pull her away from other animals' poops
- if you have a cat litter box in the house, move it to somewhere the cat reach but she can't, like on top of the washing machine.

EXERCISE AND PLAYTIME

Exercise is essential for your puppy's mental and emotional wellbeing. In the chapter on 'Exercise' we will look at how much and how often, and 'Stepping out' is full of advice and tips for safe and enjoyable outings.

Playing is just as important for a well-balanced, confident dog. It will strengthen her relationship with you as well as improving her overall social interaction. In fact playtime is so important that there's a full chapter devoted to this too, with key pointers to help you make every game and every play session a positive experience.

LEADERSHIP

For her mental health and emotional wellbeing, your puppy needs to see you, and all her human family, as her strong, clear leaders. This is never about punishment, but always about clear and consistent communication that prevents bad behaviour from developing in the first place.

Clear communication leads to mutual understanding, and a better life for your puppy as well as everyone else in the family. To achieve it, every member of the family and household must consistently use the same set of rules, spoken commands and body language.

In the chapters 'Behaviour' and 'Training' we will look at the key DOs and DON'Ts to help you build a strong foundation for a lifelong relationship based on understanding and respect.

14. ESSENTIAL CARE

When we think about a puppy's practical needs, our first thoughts are probably about food and hygiene, but before we look at those in detail, here are a few less obvious considerations.

Rest time

Puppies just sleep when they want to. Right? Not necessarily. You need to make sure your puppy has the quiet time he needs, especially if your home environment is busy and bustling. He needed 18-22 hours of rest a day when you picked him up, and by around 12 weeks he still needs a good 15 and 18 hours.

Collar

His collar fitting is also easy to forget, but he is growing fast and it'll need to be loosened regularly. Check daily that it is not getting too tight.

Over exercising

Easier said than done with an exuberant puppy, but try to minimise racing up and down stairs and jumping on and off furniture while he's growing, because his bones and joints are still firming up.

Overheating

This is worth a mention here because many dog owners don't realise how common it is for dogs to die from heatstroke, especially in cars. Dogs can't cool down by sweating like we can. Instead they pant, which is far less efficient. They should never be shut in a hot space, or any place which is likely to heat up quickly. And they should always have a ready supply of drinking water.

Dognappers

Considering the high price of puppies, dog theft is something else to be conscious of. Don't leave your puppy unattended outside for example.

FEEDING

When?

If your puppy was on four feeds a day with the breeder, then carry on with this until sometime between 12 and 16 weeks when you can cut his meals back to three times a day. Divide his daily food allowance (according to the instructions on the pack) into three portions instead of four, and alter your schedule for regular feeding to, for example, 7am, 12.30pm and 6pm. Between six and eight months, you can cut feed times back to just morning and evening, dividing the daily allowance by two.

How?

Here are some tips for this key part of his care.
- Feed him the amount stipulated on the packaging in line with his weight and age, and no more.
- You, or his primary caretaker if it's someone else, should be the person who feeds him most often.
- Keep up with some hand feeding for the few first days, or weeks even. It's a good reminder to him that you are the source of his food. It also prevents

him from turning into a growler one day when he might feel his food is under threat.

- If you have more than one dog, feed them at least six feet apart.
- Cockapoos can become fussy eaters, so to prevent this, if he doesn't eat his food, take it away after 15 minutes, and don't feed him again until his next scheduled feed.
- Aim to be consistent with meal times.
- Avoid feeding him immediately before or after exercise, and remember to avoid feeding too close to your bedtime so he's less likely to mess during the night.
- If you're eating around the same time as he is, make sure you eat first to remind him that you are at the top of the pecking order.

Change of food

You most likely started your puppy off on the diet he was having with his breeder, and it is just as likely that in time you will want to change his food. If you do, incorporate the new brand slowly, over the course of one to two weeks. For example, for two to three days give him one quarter of the daily allowance of the new food with three quarters of the daily allowance of the old. A few days later make it half of one with half of the other, again for a few days, then increase the new food to three quarters and finally the full meal.

What to feed

There's a baffling array of dog food brands and flavours on the market, so if you're making this decision without the advice of the breeder or your vet, don't skimp. With dog food you generally get what you pay for. And don't buy more than one bag at a time so that if he's lost interest in it by the end of the bag you can soon let him try another brand. It's common for dogs to be hugely enthusiastic about a particular food the first few times they try it and then suddenly change their minds. Mealtimes will always be high-points in his day, so it's only right that you shop around for a food he loves.

- Make sure you choose a food that is appropriate for his size.
- Make sure this food is also appropriate for his age – puppies need higher levels of protein, calories and nutritional supplements than adult dogs.
- Many breeders recommend a high-quality dry puppy food, so you could start by looking at the bold wording on the front of the packs. The words 'premium' and 'natural' are encouraging indicators, but legally the words 'complete' and 'balanced' are better promises of high quality. If you're in the US, look for foods endorsed by the AAFCO.

- Any food that is 'complementary' is not complete or balanced and needs to be supplemented.
- Always check the ingredients too. The main ingredient should be meat or poultry, not corn or grain.
- Avoid artificial colouring, sweeteners, sugars and salt.
- If your puppy is not faring well on commercially produced food, you could try putting him on a raw diet. This is home-prepared food – consisting mostly of raw meat, whole or crushed bones, vegetables, fruits, raw eggs and some diary – and would require a lot of extra research and work on your part.
- Luckily Cockapoos are not prone to food allergies or intolerances. But if yours does start persistently scratching, licking or chewing his legs or paws, or rubbing his face, then switching from beef to lamb, or from chicken to fish, or to a low-grain or hypoallergenic diet could help to alleviate the symptoms. If his food bowls are plastic, switching to stainless steel or ceramic could also make a difference.

TIP: Meals are good times to ask for a 'Sit' and a 'Stay' (see 'Training'). Then put his food in front of him, restraining him if necessary, wait a couple of seconds and give him the command to 'Eat up'

Overfeeding

It is important not to let your Cockapoo get overweight at any stage of his life, but it's especially important not to let him get overweight while he is still growing.

One way to manage this is to count any treats into

his daily food intake, making sure these make up no more than 10%. You could pocket some dry food from his pre-measured daily allowance to use as treats and bribes during the day. Or you might prefer to supplement his diet with carefully chosen chews and treats, but never feed these to him as scraps from the table.

Begging

The best way to avoid begging is not to let it start in the first place. Make people-food off limits from day one. Those pleading eyes are near impossible to resist, I know, but you absolutely have to be stronger than he is adorable. Never give in to him if he begs at the table, and never feed him from your plate. If begging does become a problem at mealtimes, confine him to another room until it stops.

Eight months and older

Between eight and twelve months you might want to transition your puppy's food to a 'junior' formula, but don't progress to 'adult' food until he is over a year.

GROOMING

Cockapoos love a good charge through the undergrowth gathering random samples of flora, so they can be high maintenance when it comes to grooming. Your puppy is going to need regular brushing, washing, clipping, ear cleansing and more.

Brushing

Your Cockapoo's coat could become matted or even badly tangled if it's not brushed regularly – at least once a week as a guide. But if brushing is something you enjoy, then brush away. Start a few days after bringing him home, then brush as often as you like because brushing is so much more than detangling and de-matting. It strengthens the bond between you; keeps his skin healthy; aerates his coat and helps you to pick up on any lumps, sores or parasites. It's also very good for teaching him to be handled, especially during vet visits.

Start with a brush with soft bristles and brush in the direction of hair growth. Begin at the head, and work towards the tail and down the legs. Have short sessions at first in case he's getting restless.

It's normal for him to want to mouth the brush, so be patient with him and don't give up because you think he doesn't like it. Build the time up slowly and he will soon come to love these sessions.

As he grows, you will need to take extra care to prevent matting where the coat is longest, including between his toes.

Finish a brushing session by wiping his eyes with a warm, damp cloth.

Ears

The more a dog's ears prick up, the more easily air can circulate through the ear canals. Conversely, the hairier and floppier a dog's ears, the more prone they are to infection. If your puppy has long, flat earflaps, get into the habit now of cleaning them regularly and checking for infection.

To clean the inside of his ears use a warm damp cloth, but never go deeper than you can see. And never use cotton buds. From time to time apply an ear cleansing solution as well.

Signs of infection are an unpleasant smell, crusted or dark earwax, redness or inflammation. Other indicators are more-than-usual head shaking, or scratching or rubbing of his ears. If you suspect infection, take him to the vet straight away so you can nip it in the bud. Ear infections should never be left untreated.

Going forward the insides of his ears will need trimming too to prevent the build up of dirt.

TIP: After swimming, gently dry the insides of his ears.

Washing

Cockapoos are not smelly dogs, so unless your puppy rolls in something stinky and unpleasant, try to avoid washing him more than once a month because washing strips away the natural oils that keep his skin and coat healthy.

You can use your own bath (ideally with a non-skid mat), a washtub, or even the basin or a sink. But if you're using a basin or sink, be extra careful to make sure he can't jump out and hurt himself.

- Get everything close to hand before you start. You will need a quality dog shampoo (never use people shampoo or conditioner), a sponge or cup, a soft brush, some treats and a towel. Put on old clothes and a good sense of humour, because you will get wet.
- Lift your puppy carefully into the bath or tub, offering lots of praise and treats.
- Being careful to avoid his head and ears, run lukewarm water over him. This could be with a hand-held sprayer or a cup, or with a wet sponge.
- Squeeze a drop of shampoo into your palm, smooth it onto his coat and lather (still being

careful to avoid his head and ears) then rinse several times, thoroughly working the shampoo out with your hands. (Some owners put a cotton wool ball in the ears to keep them dry through this stage of the wash, but never push them in with any pressure.)

- Last of all, clean his head, gently wiping the earflaps and inside the ears, and taking extra care not to drip water into the ear canals.
- Wrap him in a towel and rub him gently before lifting him out.
- When his coat is almost dry, give him a little brush.
- Then let him go, but don't let him outside on a cold day until he's completely dry.

TIP: If you want him to get used to the hair dryer, wrap him up in a soft towel, with just his nose sticking out. Face him away from the dryer, and blow him through the towel. NEVER use a hot setting – always cool or slightly warm, and tested on yourself first.

Trimming

Your puppy's coat won't need trimming for a while, but it wouldn't hurt for him to start getting used to the idea early on. Until he's old enough for his first proper session, you could use a pair of blunt-nosed scissors to trim the hair away from his eyes, on the insides of his ears, and between his paw pads.

There's no right or wrong age for his first full trimming, because different breed lines and coat colours grow differently. Frankly he can be clipped as soon as he's looking scruffy. You can either take him to a professional groomer, which could turn out to be as often as every two to three months, or you might prefer to invest in some clippers and learn do it yourself. With a Cockapoo you are aiming for the teddy-bear look with a trim that is 2-3" long all over.

Nails

Your puppy's nails impact directly on how he walks, so they must be kept short. You might find that exercise on pavements and hard ground wears them down naturally, but any time they do get unmanageably long they will need to be trimmed.

Vets and dog groomers can do this for you but if your puppy's nails need doing as often as every month or two, it would pay off in the long run to buy your own dog nail trimming clippers – which are specially designed to prevent over-trimming – and learn to do it yourself.

Clipping is obviously not something you can practice every day, but what you can do often is help your puppy to get used to the idea. Choose times when he is already relaxed, then take hold of his paw and tap his nails gently with the clippers. When he responds calmly, praise him or give him a treat.

The next stage is to hold his paw and clasp a nail in the clippers – without making the clip but still showering him with praise when he stays calm. You might want to get someone to hold him for you when you do this.

When you are ready to make the cut you want to avoid the 'quick', which is inside the nail and contains sensitive nerve endings. If the nails are white or light in colour, you should be able to see the pink of the quick quite clearly. If they are dark, however, clip a tiny bit at a time (no more than a millimetre), inspecting after each clip to make sure there is no bleeding.

If necessary, do no more than one or two nails at a time, praising him after each session, then making a note of the ones you've done.

If he has dew claws – the nails on the upper, inner part of his feet – then don't forget to trim these too. (If he doesn't have these, don't worry. Some breeders will have had them removed soon after birth.)

If you want, you can file the nails smooth with an emery board.

Do nail trimming often so that you won't have to cut much off at any one time, and soon your puppy will be comfortable with the process.

Teeth

There are lots of treats on the market that double as dental chews to clean your puppy's teeth and keep his gums healthy. However, if you want to clean his teeth by brushing you will need dog toothbrushes and meat-flavoured pastes. There are plenty of 'How to' videos online.

Fleas and ticks

To prevent ticks and fleas, it's worth using a vet-recommended treatment, but never before your puppy is 12 weeks old.

If he does get fleas, wash him as usual, combing him while wet with a fine-toothed flea comb. After each brush, rinse the comb in hot, soapy water. Then wash his bedding, and clean and vacuum the house thoroughly to get rid of any unhatched eggs.

If you find a tick, don't panic. It happens. But don't just pull it out either. Cover it with petroleum jelly which will suffocate it and force it to release its hold. Wait five minutes, then pluck it off using tweezers or your nails, from as close to the skin as possible to make sure the head doesn't stay behind.

15. BEHAVIOUR

Your puppy loves you so much! She wants to learn from you and please you. But she only knows what her survival instincts tell her, so, to reiterate, it's your job to teach her what is and isn't allowed in your world. We will look at specific behaviours in the next chapters, but the pointers in this general chapter are fundamental to every one of them.

For a well-behaved puppy, the first thing to understand – as I'm sure you do by now – is that puppies are much more receptive when they have nothing to fear. A fearful puppy will never be totally engaged.

Our understanding of animal behaviour is improving all the time, and it's no longer acceptable to punish dogs, never mind puppies, by shouting, smacking and rubbing their noses in the carpet. This sort of treatment is not just archaic, it's also ineffective and counterproductive. It scares your puppy and puts you in a bad mood. You lose your dog's trust and the spinout of that – into all the other areas of the relationship – is just not worth thinking about. You want your puppy to be happy and optimistic, looking forward to everything, rather than fearing it.

So how do you achieve this? In a nutshell: you gain her trust by focusing on the things she does right. By encouraging good behaviour and rewarding it.

Encourage and reward

Always tell her what you DO want her to do, rather than what you DON'T want her to do. If she's got the TV remote between her teeth, don't shout and get angry. Calmly distract her with something else, something she IS allowed to chew on. Refocus her on this new and exciting treat or toy, and rescue the remote. If you don't have anything at hand, then ask her to do something to obey you – even something as simple as a 'Sit!'

Then, when she IS doing something you DO want her to do, say 'Yes' or 'Good puppy' in a happy and positive voice. And if there's a treat at hand, treat her immediately.

TIP: If your treat-bribes start losing their appeal, look for better, tastier ones.

Her feelings are everything

Let's say your puppy bounces up to you with a glint in her eye, a waggle in her tail and a captured, disheveled bathmat in her mouth. Try not to think about your favourite bathmat which, after all, is just a thing and

has no feelings at all! Instead, think about HOW SHE'S FEELING about what she's done. She thinks she's done brilliantly, doesn't she? She wants a medal. Scold her now and you'll really confuse her. Then again, if you praise her, she might keep bringing you bathmat-type presents ad infinitum. So what do you do?

You don't scold or praise. Distract her instead by calling her to you and getting her attention onto something else, a toy perhaps. When she is refocused on the toy, offer her a tempting chew. By then the bathmat should be far from her mind, and you should be able to rescue it. And if it's still fit-for-purpose, remember to hang it up out of her puppy-jaw reach for a few months.

Prevent bad behaviour

- Don't put temptation in her way. If you don't want her eating from your dinner plate, don't leave it lying around, unattended and in easy reach. That would just be setting her up to fail.
- Try to anticipate things that might go wrong. If you think she's about to chase the cat, hold on to her and distract her with a toy. Dangling tablecloths, for example, are begging for trouble. Don't use them until she's older.
- Make sure her basic needs are met: love, food, water, warmth, things to chew on, sleep, play, exercise and exploration. If she has all of these she is far less likely to behave badly in the first place.

Ignore her when you disapprove

With many bad behaviours, the best way to tell your puppy you don't like what she's doing is to take away something she wants. Your attention. So to discourage bad behaviour, ignore her when she's doing anything that is not acceptable to you.

- Don't chase after her when she's taken something she shouldn't have.
- Don't yell at her when she doesn't come.
- Don't push her off if she jumps up on you or others.

Ignore her, and make it as obvious as you can: stop playing, walk away, fold your arms, look away, even leave the room if you can.

You are the leader

To establish a positive relationship, your puppy must understand from the start that, even though you love her to the proverbial moon and back, and you are best friends, your word is law and she must listen to you. And she will, as long as you are a worthy leader and a good teacher.

Here are some key tips and reminders.

- Don't be aggressive towards her. Instead, be gentle but firm.
- Don't go too easy on her either. In the long run that can be as unfair as punishing her.
- Be crystal clear in your instructions. Use single words rather than sentences and try to be consistent in your choice of words. Don't switch between 'Come!' and 'Here!' for example, or 'Walk!' and 'Heel!'
- Keep your tone positive.
- Use body language as well as verbal commands.
- When she does what you want, show her unreservedly how clever she is. Be happy and excited and reward her with praise.

Alpha dog issues and the bed v crate debate

It's highly likely that your puppy, clever as she no doubt is, will soon decide your bed is the most comfortable place in the world, and that cuddling up there, nice and close to you, is the best and safest way to spend the nights. So while we're on leadership, it's worth noting that letting your puppy sleep on your bed could serve to undermine your top place in the pack. In the wild, being able to choose the best sleeping spot, especially when it is high up, is the privilege of the alpha dog, so even if you do decide to let her sleep there, be sure to let her know where she is and isn't allowed.

Rules must be consistent

I know, I know, we've been here before, but this is really important. If one person lets your puppy onto the sofa, it's downright unfair for someone else to reprimand her for being there. Rules will be very confusing if they differ from person to person, so it's really crucial that everyone in your puppy's life understands and teaches what is and what isn't allowed using the same set of rules, spoken commands and body language.

Timing is all-important

It's vital that you teach your puppy with timely signals too – signals that apply to what she is doing AT THAT TIME. If you try to tell her off for something she did two minutes ago, she won't understand what she's done wrong. For example, if she runs off after a cat and then comes back, and you shout at her for chasing the cat as she is coming back, she will think you are shouting at her for coming back and not for chasing the cat. The result? She will be confused and intimidated, and next time she will think twice about coming back. Too many well-meaning dog owners make the mistake of misplaced timing – and it's simply unfair.

When to say 'No!' or 'Leave!'

There will be times when you absolutely do need to tell her her behaviour is unacceptable. For example, if she is doing something that could endanger her or cause harm to someone else. This also applies when she brazenly ignores your command because she would rather do something else.

These need to be corrected immediately and here's how.

- Reprimand her straight away. Say 'NO!' or 'LEAVE!' in your emergency voice – a voice that is so much louder and sharper than your usual quiet and calm voice, that it startles her enough to prevent or stop her behaviour. Use this voice sparingly for best effect.
- Block her way with your body, or physically stop her if you need to.
- Then make eye contact and use your voice to get her to focus on you.
- Once you have her attention, praise her for changing her focus.
- 'No' and 'Leave' are never enough on their own because your puppy doesn't know what she's meant to do instead. Always try to give her something else to do or to chew on.

Still struggling?

If you've tried all these things with a bad behaviour, with repeated, clear and consistent communication, and you're still struggling, you can resort to time-out. Shut her in the kitchen, or a similar and safe place (NOT her crate or special place), and leave her for a few minutes – five is acceptable, ten is too long.

Serious behavioural problems

These include incessant barking, aggression and destructive chewing. But all problems are caused by something, be it boredom, loneliness, lack of socialisation, lack of training, fear, anxiety or insecurity, being spoilt or badly treated, or even just poor breeding.

With serious problems, it is especially important that you are able to tell the difference between playfulness and aggression. See the chapter 'Puppy-People Translator' for clues on reading the signs. If your puppy develops any traits that could endanger you, herself, or any other person or their dog, you should get help from a professional in dog behaviour. And the same goes for any other serious behavioural problem.

The following chapters (right up to 'Training') focus on the specific challenges you are most likely to face with your new Cockapoo puppy, and are filled with tips to help you as you guide her into adolescence and beyond.

16. TOILET TRAINING

With Poodle intelligence and the Cocker Spaniel's acute sense of smell and eagerness to please, Cockapoos tend to be quicker and easier to housetrain than the average breed. They are clean dogs and your puppy won't want to soil his bed.

But no-one said housetraining was easy. At first your puppy will have no idea that his new home is not a public toilet. This is something you need to teach him, with time and patience.

In a nutshell, initially you will need to take him outside hourly and show him where to go. When he does go in an acceptable place, and as soon as he has finished his business, it's time to celebrate. Reward! Reward! Reward! That way you will teach him that doing his business in that place means AMAZING things will happen.

Here are some tips and key DOs and DON'Ts to help speed up the process.

Agree on where

Decide as a family or household on the outside patch or area you'd most like him to use for his business, and this is where you should lead him every toilet time. He will instinctively look for somewhere absorbent, like a patch of grass, but if you're lawn proud you'll soon learn that lawn and piddles are not a good combination, so if there's a suitable place with soft sand or gravel, encourage him to go there instead. (If that doesn't work, don't despair. There are plenty of piddle-patch repair products on the market.)

Do

- When you bring your puppy inside for the first time, give him a guided tour of the house. The sooner he understands that all this space is living area, the sooner he will stop using it as a toilet.
- Take him to your chosen piddle patch hourly, including as soon as he wakes, and within 15 minutes of finishing a meal.
- Also take him there immediately if you spot any of these tell-tale signs:
  - Sniffing and circling the floor
  - Pacing up and down
  - Looking towards or sitting at the door to the toilet area
  - Scratching the floor.
- Then wait. And wait some more. Stay with him – come rain or shine – watching him all the time.
- You can spur him on with an encouraging command, like 'piddle now' or 'wee time'.
- Wait until he's completely finished before you reward him, or he might only do half his business.
- As soon as he's finished, shower him with praise.

Don't

- Punish him for piddling or pooping inside. Punishing him for something he can't help and doesn't fully understand would only make him nervous and slow his progress.

- Leave him outside (or in a piddle spot) on his own. He will instinctively turn his attention to getting back to you, and when he does get back, he will very likely still need to go.

Tips
- When he goes to the toilet in the house, thoroughly clean the place he's marked and use a pet-safe odour eliminator. This is because next time he goes to the toilet he's likely to choose somewhere he can already smell wee or poop.
- If he has messed inside but on a training mat or piece of newspaper, carry this outside to where you'd like him to go, and weigh it down there with something heavy. The smell will act as a signal to him to do his business there next time.
- If you're taking him outside during the night just pick him up, take him out, put him on his piddle patch and say 'wee time' or whatever words you've chosen. Don't talk to him or fuss over him and if he gets playful, ignore him or it will be difficult for him to settle back down.
- Cockapoos are particularly good with bell training, which is ringing a bell or a string of bells to let you know when they need to go out. Make your own, or buy one from a pet store, and hang it from the door that leads to outside. Then 'paw' it yourself whenever you are specifically taking your puppy outside for toilet time – never when you are going out for a play. Once your puppy understands that you want him to do his toiletries outside, he will soon learn to jingle the bells himself to tell you when he needs to go out.

How long will toilet training take?

The average medium-sized Cockapoo is pretty much there by four to five months, but progress varies from puppy to puppy. Small dogs take longer to toilet train than bigger ones, so if your puppy's Poodle mix is Toy, its progress is likely to be slower than that of a Cockapoo puppy bred from a Standard. It's safe to assume your puppy will leave the odd surprise for you until he's around six months, and it could take up to a year for him to be accident free.

NOTE: Some dogs make a little wee as a sign of submission, and some wee with excitement. These lapses should never be punished!

17. CHEWING HOUSE AND HOME

Cockapoos are retrievers on both sides of their ancestry, and all retrievers are mouthy. They were bred to carrying things around in their mouths and, especially as puppies, they love nothing more than a good chew on those things while they're at it. But all puppies chew. They don't have hands, so chewing is how they explore and learn about the world around them. They inspect everything they can with their mouths and teeth.

They also chew because they are teething. By twelve weeks, your Cockapoo's adult teeth, a full 42 of them, are waiting to push out those super-sharp baby teeth. It then takes until around 16 weeks for those baby teeth to even start falling out, and the teething process goes on until she is around eight to ten months. Imagine her frustration. That's a lot of weeks of important but uncomfortable chewing to be done, so for the sake of your puppy, your house and your sanity, keep valuables out of reach.

Your puppy will chew on anything she can during this time. Be understanding, and always have an abundant supply of toys and treats at hand that she IS allowed to chew on.

Don't

- Leave valuable and tempting chewables, like shoes, lying on the floor. Anything left lying around is fair game. Puppies are excellent training for untidy owners.

- Don't leave supposedly less-tempting valuables lying around either. Things like sunglasses, mobile phones and even car keys.
- Don't encourage sticks. They can splinter and get stuck in her mouth.
- If you find your puppy with something she shouldn't have, don't try to force it away from her. If it's small enough, she might decide to swallow it rather than give it up.
- And certainly don't start a tug-of-war.

Do

- Instead of trying to pull or coax a forbidden object from her, offer her something she **is** allowed to chew on – a replacement item she'll want even more than whatever she's got.
  As she plays with the forbidden item, hold

the new and better offering to her nose and say, 'Leave!', 'Drop!' or 'Off!'.

- When she drops it, you can give her the treat and a pat.
- Make sure you have an abundant supply of tempting puppy treats and toys. (Pet toys are created to appeal to your dog by smell, taste, feel and shape.)
- Keep these temptations close by. You never know when you'll be needing them.
- If you see your puppy approaching something with demolition on her mind, call her with a happy voice. Puppies are easily distracted, and she should immediately forget what she'd planned to do and come running to you. Reward her for coming and give her something more suitable to get her teeth into.
- If she's got a taste for something that can't be moved, a table leg for example, spray it with a pet-friendly anti-chew, or citronella.
- If you suspect she has eaten something harmful, call the vet immediately.

Chewing is an essential phase in every puppy's development, and it carries on for months. Hang in there because her need to gnaw on everything in sight **will** lessen. It just won't happen overnight.

TEETHING TIPS

- *Tie a knot in an old cloth, wet it and put it in the freezer. Then give it to her when it is frozen to ease her sore gums.*

- *Give her a chilled or frozen carrot to chew on.*

18. MOUTHING AND NIPPING

All puppies love to play, and playing for all dogs involves mouthing one another, so it's completely natural for your puppy to want to play bite. He might also bite because he's teething. It's possible that, like many new puppy owners, you don't mind your puppy chewing your hands now, but you soon will. As he gets older, the biting will get harder and involve others too, so it's important that he learns as soon as possible not to use his teeth on people.

Adult dogs are good at controlling the pressure of their jaws, but puppies often make the mistake of biting too hard because they are still learning and practising jaw control. Your puppy has already learned from the other puppies in his litter that biting inhibits play time. If a puppy had bitten one of its litter mates too hard, the hurt puppy would have yelped and stopped playing.

With you too, he will gradually learn to play more gently until he understands not to let his teeth into contact with your skin at all.

Do

- Play with him with a chew toy in your hand. If he bites you and inflicts pain, make a high yelping sound and immediately withdraw your hand. Because this is exactly what would have happened with his litter mates, it will help him to learn that it's okay to nip the chew toy, but not your hand.

- If the biting persists, remove yourself from the game, the room even, just for a few minutes to show him that teeth on skin equals no more playing. It's not a quick fix, but he will gradually make the association.
- Supervise small children. Their tendency when a puppy mouths them is to scream and run around, which only excites and encourages the puppy even more.

Don't

- Shout at him or smack him if he mouths or nips. This can make the biting harder to control.
- Rush his progress. He must learn jaw control gradually and through experience.
- Play rough tug games – they just encourage biting.

19. JUMPING UP

Cockapoos are always happy and excited to see people, so it's entirely natural for them to want to leap up against you, and others too. Your adoring puppy will jump up because he's happy to see you, because he loves you, because he wants to lick you all over your face and he can't reach, because he wants you to pet him and play with him.

He is used to jumping up on his mother and litter mates, but he needs to learn not to jump up on you or other people. Right now, while he's little, you mightn't mind his jumping up, but a large, fully grown Cockapoo could bowl someone right over with sheer exuberance. And size aside, don't forget about those muddy paws and sharp claws. Basically, jumping up soon becomes a nuisance and you want to nip it in the bud before it gets out of hand. So when he jumps up, and he will, don't:

- reward him
- talk to him or tell him to get down
- push him away
- shout or yell
- smack him or use physical punishment of any sort.

Instead

- Step back so that his paws don't reach you
- Look away from him

- Turn away from him
- Lift your hands away and don't touch him
- After a few seconds, come back to him, and repeat if necessary
- When he has quietened down and stopped jumping, be sure to praise him and reward him.
- Get all the family to do this, and ask regular visitors to help with it too.
- If jumping up on visitors is likely, put him on a lead before opening the door to them.

How does it work?

These methods will eventually teach him that if he jumps up he will get no attention, and that if he keeps his four paws on the ground he will be praised.

20. DIGGING

Not all Cockapoos dig, but if your puppy turns out to be a digger remember that she can't differentiate between the compost heap and your newly planted flowerbeds. So don't get cross with her. Instead, try to understand **why** she's digging, so you can address it effectively.

Digging can be for any number of reasons and luckily, the most likely of these is for the pure fun of it – she's fit to bursting with excess energy and has found a happy way to burn it off. The best response in this case is probably to tire her out. Try increasing her daily exercise. Take longer walks, increase playtimes and distract her with more toys.

Better still, you could embrace her digging. Make it even more fun.

- Create an area that's just for her – a place where she **is** allowed to dig, and to her heart's content. Make or buy her a sandpit if necessary.
- Bury things there for her to find.
- Then, if you find her digging in other places, tell her 'No!' or 'Leave!', refill the holes she has made, and show her again where she can and should dig instead.

Other reasons she might be digging are because she's got scent of something of 'utmost importance' under the ground, or she's found something top secret that needs burying. In these cases, her digging will be persistently in the same seemingly random spot. And if this is a problem, your best response is simply to close her access to the area. Keep her away or fence it off for a while.

The most serious digging, however, is digging that is always at the boundary of your garden or yard. If your puppy begins this type of digging, she is probably trying to get out, and most likely because she is looking for companionship. You would need to tackle this immediately, and in two ways: by making absolutely sure your property is still escape-proof, and by addressing possible loneliness. (See the chapter 'Separation Anxiety'.)

SOMETHING TO TRY
If her digging becomes a real problem try making an unpleasant clanging noise. Rattle some coins in a tin or hit a pot with a metal spoon until she associates her digging in that place with this horrible noise.

21. BARKING

All dogs bark and your Cockapoo will too. She will bark for good reason, for no reason at all, just for fun, to make suggestions or even to make demands. In fact, she's likely to invent her own box-full of sound tricks, and every one will have its own distinct meaning. Listen to her and you'll soon learn to tell the difference between them. Some are necessary and some are cute, but others can be, or will soon become, downright annoying. And those need to be nipped in the bud.

Barking at you

As your puppy comes to see that her efforts to win your attention, like jumping up or nipping, are fruitless, she's likely to start replacing these with her latest greatest trick – a demanding bark noise that says: 'I am still here', 'Stop ignoring me', 'I want some of that too' or 'Come on, let's play.'

Whatever it is, she wants your attention. Don't give it to her. Instead, pull out your now-well-practiced ignoring techniques.

- Look away and turn away
- Don't talk to her
- Lift your hands away and don't touch her
- Leave the room if you can
- But, as always, as soon as she has quietened down, be sure to acknowledge and reward her.

Barking at others

Most Cockapoos will welcome everyone into the house with their tails wagging 19 to the dozen. It's no secret they don't make good guard dogs. But before the door is opened, they could well bark to warn you of the new and possibly suspicious arrival, and that kind of barking is not necessarily something you want to stop or even discourage. Let her bark, just momentarily, then say 'Quiet!' or 'Hush' in a soft voice, call her back to you and praise her, or distract her with a toy or a treat if you need to.

If your puppy is barking at the neighbour's cat – which is more likely at this stage – and you want her to stop straight away, your instinct might be to shout at her to keep quiet. But put yourself in her shoes and you will see that if you shout at her while she is barking, she could think you're egging her on, or even coming to help. The result? She would bark even harder.

So with nuisance barking, as with pretty much all bad behaviour, it is more effective to give her the 'I'm ignoring you now!' treatment, or to distract her – say 'Quiet!' or 'Hush' in your soft voice and treat her when she has settled down for a few seconds. Keep treating her if you need to because she simply can't sniff and bark at the same time.

TIP: If the barking persists, you could try distracting her with a loud noise. Hit a pot with a metal spoon for example.

If she's barking at other dogs while out on the lead, it is more likely out of fear than aggression. Get her focus on you, ask for something, a Sit for example, then treat her, calm her down, and show her you're not afraid.

Barking to communicate a need

Sometimes barking is a genuine plea for help. Perhaps she needs to go outside for the toilet. Maybe something is truly scaring her. Really listen to her and ask yourself why she might be barking. Consider what is going on around her at the time and you will soon learn the difference between attention-seeking barks and barks that express a real need. A higher-pitched bark, for example, is often an indication of fear.

Problem barking

This is when nuisance barking, which is annoying but intermittent, becomes incessant and unbearable. It is never without reason. For example, if a puppy is left on her own for long periods, shut in a small space, or trying not to relieve herself inside, she WILL bark. In fact, she will probably howl. And who could blame her? Wherever barking is linked to a genuine need, it is the need that needs addressing, rather than the barking, so try to find out what's setting her off in the first place. The most common causes are loneliness, frustration, boredom or lack of attention, and here are some things you could try.

Do

- Make sure she isn't barking because she feels threatened by anything.
- Take her for longer walks.
- Give her more time to interact with you and other dogs.
- If she's alone (even in another room):
  - move her to a less isolated place
  - arrange for there to be more space for her to play in

- leave more toys for her to play with.
- If she has to be left alone for a long stretch while you are out:
  - arrange for someone to come and walk her or play with her
  - if this will be a regular occurrence, consider getting another dog for company.

Don't
- Leave your puppy alone for a long time without arranging extra care, a dog walker for example, and definitely not in a small space. It's simply not fair.

Getting serious

If you've been consistent, persistent and patient with your puppy's socialisation and training and she is still barking incessantly and for no apparent reason, you might need extra help. There are methods you can try and products you can buy, but most of them punish barking rather than reinforcing positive behaviour, so it would be better in the long run to consult a dog behaviour expert who can come to your home.

22. SEPARATION ANXIETY

This is the fear of being alone.

Few dogs cope well on their own and Cockapoos are no exception. They are commonly referred to as Velcro dogs for their need to stick right by your side, and consequently they suffer anxiety through separation. All Cockapoos are susceptible to separation anxiety – it is arguably their only weakness – but smaller Cockapoos bred from Toy Poodles are more likely to suffer than those from the bigger strains.

Separation anxiety can show in a multitude of negative behaviours, including barking, whining, pacing, digging and scratching, self-licking, destructive chewing, loss of bowel and bladder control, throwing up, refusing to eat or drink, and even desperate excitement at your return. Repeatedly left alone for long stretches, a Cockapoo will easily suffer from any or many of these, so don't get one if you're going to be out at work all day.

But of course there will be some times when you do have to leave your puppy alone, even for very short stretches. It's inevitable. So let's look at what can be done now, at the puppy stage, to prevent anxiety from developing.

Your puppy will quickly learn when you're about to go out from the indications you give him – like putting on your shoes, fetching your bag or picking up the keys – and the anxiety will start to kick in as soon as he picks up on these signs. He won't want you to leave, so he'll most likely start following you, jumping up on you and seeking your attention in any way he can.

So, what to do? First of all **never** punish him for showing signs of distress at your leaving. He's not being naughty, but this behaviour makes it all the more important that you manage leaving him with care and planning.

First steps

Do your leaving-the-house things often and from day one, even when you're not going anywhere – things like picking up your keys, walking outside and coming straight back in again. This will go a long way to helping him cope with your future comings and goings.

It is wise to start leaving him on his own from early on, for just a few minutes a day, so he understands quickly that this is normal and there is nothing to worry about. But before actually going out for the first time, make sure he's had time to really bond with you.

- Then decide on a special place to leave him, in his crate or a playpen for example, and fill it with everything he needs: bedding, water, food, wee mat. Keep the space small and den-like because this will help him to feel safe. (Giving him free rein in a big house would leave him feeling exposed and even more alone.)
- Next include some distraction toys or treats – items that will keep him so engrossed that he forgets to be worried about being alone. Toys filled with

slow-release treats are ideal, like a Kong stuffed with something as wonderfully yummy as it is difficult to get at. Poached liver or chicken are irresistible, as is peanut butter (but make sure it doesn't contain Xylitol). There's a remarkable range of products on the market that double as separation anxiety aids, including:

- ○ interactive toys that respond to touch with squeaking or even speaking
- ○ companion toys – stuffed animal toys that mimic the heartbeat and body warmth of another dog
- ○ pet cams which enable you to monitor your puppy and even flick him treats via an app on your smartphone.

- With his place and distractions planned, choose a time when he's getting tired and likely to sleep soon, after a walk or an exciting playtime for example.
- Make sure he's had a toilet break.
- Put him in his 'den', ignore any whining and leave the room or go out for a short while (five to ten minutes).
- When you get back, don't make an unusually big fuss of him. Be as matter of fact about it as you can.
- If he's asleep when you return, don't disturb him. Quietly open the crate door or puppy gate so he can get out when he wakes.

Lengthening the separation

When you start leaving him for longer periods, do it very, very gradually, building up to no more than an hour until he is around six months. For one thing, he will be needing the toilet.

Leaving him for a long time

Ideally don't do it. But going forward there could be times when you are left with no choice. Here are some ideas to minimise the stress.

- Drop him off with a responsible family member, friend or dog-sitter.
- Ask a neighbour or pay a pet-sitter to come and spend some time with him, or employ a dog walker.
- Take him for a decent walk before you set off. Exercise has a calming effect, and he'll be more likely to have a sleep when you leave.
- Make sure he has everything he needs, including fresh water and plenty of toys.
- Consider the changes in temperature while you're out. For example, you might've left him in a confined space with a lovely window view, but this might also mean he is trapped in glaring sunlight later in the day.
- You could leave soothing music playing in the house. Some soundtracks are created specifically for keeping dogs calm and comforted.
- If it's likely to be dark when you get home, leave a light on.

TIPS

- *Never punish your puppy for misbehaving while you were out.*

- *Make sure all the other members of the household spend time with him too – feeding him, walking him, playing with him and handling him – so he doesn't become overly dependent on one person.*

23. STEPPING OUT

Apart from being snuggled up with you, there's just one other place your growing and adult Cockapoo will want to be, and that is outdoors – ideally off the lead. But first, the baby steps …

You can only start walking your puppy out and taking him on outings once he has been fully vaccinated, and once he has had some practice walking on the lead at home. Luckily, while you're waiting for his vaccinations to take effect is the ideal time to practise this lead training.

Eventually all that you want is for him to walk nicely by your side on a loose lead. Sounds simple enough. But with his seemingly endless stores of pent-up energy, this is surprisingly difficult for a puppy to learn.

Do
- Start with a collar or a harness and a short, non-extendable lead.
- Attach the lead when he is calm and not resisting you.
- Then let him wander around the house with the lead trailing behind him, but try not to let him chew it.
- The next stage is to pick up the lead and encourage him to walk along beside you.

- When he is walking nicely alongside you, with the lead slack but off the ground, reward him generously with praise and treats.

Don't
- Drag him. That would only make him panic and pull away.
- If he is pulling, don't be pulled along by him. That would teach him that pulling works in his favour. But don't pull back either, or yank on the lead or shout at him. Instead, stop and call him to you. Praise him when he comes, then try again.

When your puppy is ready for his first walks out, these are a few things to consider and be aware of.

Where and when

Think carefully about where you're going to take him and when, so you can avoid frightening or stressful experiences.

- Choose a safe, open space away from busy roads.
- Choose a place where other dog owners are likely to act in a responsible way.
- And think about the best time to go. Perhaps it's too soon for a Saturday morning at the park if there is likely to be a noisy sports match in play.

What to take

As well as your puppy in his collar or harness and the non-extendable lead, you will need:

- Poo(p) bags – more than one
- Treats (ideally in a treat pouch) – so you can reward good behaviour
- Water and a bowl – if there is no clean water where you are going.

TIP: As a space saver, you might like to invest in a pet water bottle with a flap or lid that doubles as a bowl.

Out and about

- Give him time to sniff at things. He will love exploring new scents.
- Use this time to practice good behaviour and commands.
- If something scares him, let him know you are there with him, protecting him, and that he is safe.

But resist picking him up unless it's a real threat because you want to encourage independence.

- Walking out comes with its own risks – some obvious and others totally unpredictable. Beware of other animals, dogs included, and be careful what he might find to eat, for example tasty plants that mightn't be safe.

Pooping

If he poops, pick it up with a poo(p) bag and dispose of it at home (or in a public dog waste bin if one is provided).

Other dogs

When you come across other dogs on your outings, you could use the opportunity for your puppy to practise his meeting and greeting. But never assume that other people or their dogs are happy to reciprocate. And never let your puppy run up to other dogs unless their walkers have told you it's okay. There are lots of reasons why it might not be. Perhaps the dog is very old; maybe it is injured; in recovery; not good with puppies; or the owner is working on a specific training exercise. Always ask first and from a distance:

1. whether their dog is good with puppies and
2. whether they are happy for your puppy to say 'hello'.

If it is okay for your dogs to meet, stay close by to supervise, and to pre-empt any bad experiences.

Make sure you walk on past some dogs, and people too, so your puppy doesn't take it for granted that he can run up to anyone for a chin- and tail-wag.

Play dates

If your puppy meets another dog he plays especially well with, you could arrange play dates at times that suit you both.

Together time

- Put your phone out of temptation's way and make this quality time with your puppy!
- If you're going somewhere with big open spaces you might prefer to take an extendable lead. But be extra careful because you have far less control with these. And NEVER pull your puppy back with the line. He should come to you when you call him. There is more on this in 'Training'.

Coming off the lead

When your puppy's very young, he's utterly dependent on you, and much more likely to stay close by your side than he will be in a few weeks or months when he's grown in stature and confidence. For this reason, it's advisable to start letting him off the lead as soon as you're comfortable. This should be for very short stretches to start with, and in safe and carefully chosen places – away from traffic, other dogs and any other conceivable dangers. Chances are high that he'll stay close to you, and you'll soon be able to gauge how much free rein you can safely give him.

In the chapter on 'Training' we will look at Recall, which is teaching your puppy to come to you when you call him. Practice this at home before letting him off the lead when you're out and about.

24. EXERCISE

Now let's look at how much exercise to give your puppy through her growing up months, as well as when, where and how.

How much?

This will depend on her energy levels, temperament and ancestry. And because Cockapoos are highly adaptable, it will also depend on your lifestyle and what she gets used to, living with you. It's safe to say that as an adult, she will need a minimum of an hour's exercise a day, spread over at least two sessions. But until she is around 18 months old, she is a growing puppy, and her bones and joints are still firming up, so her exercise should be limited.

As a guide, at between eight and 11 weeks take her on two walks a day of no more than 10-15 minutes at a time. Then add five minutes to the length of each walk per month of age. On this basis:

- by four months she should be getting 20 minutes of exercise, twice a day.
- by six months she should be getting 30 minutes of exercise twice a day, or you could split this into three sessions of 20 minutes each.
- by nine months to a year, she should ideally be getting a good 45 minutes to an hour of exercise morning and evening. If, with that, you find she is

bored, destructive or putting on weight, you can increase the amount.

Until she is fully grown, she should not be going on long hikes.

TIP: As a rule, more shorter walks are better for puppies than fewer longer ones.

When to exercise

Ideally this should be once early in the day, and then again in the afternoon or evening. Cockapoos thrive on routine, so choose exercise and playtimes and stick to them as closely as possible. But avoid exercising immediately before or after eating, or within an hour of her bedtime.

TIP: If you will be walking her in the dark, invest in a high-vis jacket or a collar with flashing lights.

Walking

This is fantastic, low-impact exercise for you both. Once your puppy is walking nicely on the lead, you can start picking up the pace, gradually working up to a brisker walk and over longer distances.

Remember she is not 'booted' like you, so be mindful of her paws if the ground surface could be either very hot, or cold and icy.

Running

When she's fully grown your Cockapoo could make a wonderful running partner (see the chapter 'Going forward'). But **never** jog with your puppy. Her bones are still forming.

Games and playtime

These also count towards your puppy's daily exercise and are fantastic for mental stimulation. Cockapoos are natural retrievers, so if you want to make your puppy very happy, throw some toys for her to chase and fetch. The chapter 'Playtime' is filled with ideas and tips.

Swimming

Poodles were originally bred as water dogs and most Cocker Spaniels take to the water like ducks, so unsurprisingly Cockapoos often love water and they can be good little swimmers. Nevertheless ALWAYS supervise, and don't push your puppy into anything she doesn't want to do.

The exception is if there's a real need for your puppy to learn to swim, say for example you often walk along a riverside. Then, start her somewhere with a gradual incline into the water and go in with her. She might try to walk on the water at first, lifting her front feet right out with each step. If she does this, hold her bottom up so that her front feet stay underwater.

If she walks in on her own, then stops before she loses contact with the bottom, you could support her under her ribcage, keeping her level until she gets the hang of it.

If you have a pool, you must teach her where the shallowest step or exit is and how to get there. The best way to do this is to lift her into this part of the pool with you and show her how to jump out. Gradually she can learn to get back to the step (or exit point) from further away.

Always stay right by her side, ready and watching, guarding and guiding.

When she is older you can throw a ball or a stick into the water for her to fetch, and she is likely to play at this happily for hours. But swimming is more tiring for her than walking or running, so it's up to you to gauge when it's time to stop.

After swim times, dry the insides of her ears gently but well.

BUT

All of these activities come with their own risks – some obvious and others totally unpredictable, so here is a shortlist of things to be alert to. This is not meant to have you deprive your puppy or dog of the great outdoors and the exercise she absolutely must have; it's simply to help you avoid taking chances with her safety.

On land

- Even if your puppy or dog is hugely reliable off the lead, blind trust is still careless. Don't let her loose anywhere near traffic – she can cover a lot of ground very quickly and animals like birds, squirrels and rabbits could lure her away on a merry chase.

- Make sure you know the area well before letting her off the lead – apart from roads, be aware of cliffs, drainage culverts and thin ice.
- Be careful not to let her 'graze' on greenery on walks. Not all tasty plants are agreeable, or even safe.
- If you've been in long grass in the summer months, check her for grass seeds after walks, being extra thorough when checking her paws and ears. Grass seeds are arrow-shaped with pointy ends which attach themselves to your dog's fur. They can pierce the skin, cause all manner of irritation and even lead to infection.

In snow

De-icing products like salt and grit can contain chemicals that are harmful to dogs. So if you walk your Cockapoo on roads and pavements that might've been treated, you will need to wash her paws as soon as you get home. Also wash off any ice or snow balls from her legs, ears and tummy, but only use lukewarm water. It should never be hot.

If your dog will be spending lots of time in snow, apply a quality paw wax to her paws or try her in dog boots. (Choose ones with a velcro fastening at the back as they tend to stay on better than most.)

In water

As a basic rule, if your puppy is swimming take the same precautions with her as you would with a young child.

- Very cold water can cause hypothermia, which could drain her of her strength to swim to land.
- In the sea, stay clear of rough waves, undertows and side currents.
- Rivers are dangerous when they are fast-flowing, eddying or moving towards a waterfall or weir.
- Be especially careful of steep banks – natural drops as well as manmade ones like ditches and canals; anything she couldn't easily get out of.
- If it's a swimming pool she's in, make sure she knows how to get out.
- In open waters, consider the possibility of other animals: alligators, crocs, snapping turtles.

After the action

Cockapoos can be supremely bouncy and over-active, but after a wholesome workout your puppy will most likely be instantly and blissfully happy to settle quietly by your side.

25. TRAINING

You probably think puppy training is about training your puppy – most people do – but in fact it is nearly all about you, learning how to communicate effectively with your newest member of the family.

Training is all about improved communication and understanding, so think of every minute as an investment in a better quality of life for you, your puppy … and everyone she meets.

Everything from the chapter on Behaviour applies to this chapter too because the premise for training is the same. Because your puppy is more engaged when she has nothing to fear, you should train by encouraging and rewarding good behaviour. Always tell her what you DO want her to do, rather than what you DON'T want her to do.

And training should be fun. The best trained dogs wag their tails during training because they are loving the challenge as much as the reward.

Reward-based training

Praise is always a motivator in training, but it is often not enough, and it is now commonly accepted that training with food-motivation, at least at first, has the best results. Luckily, you're already ahead of the game with a Cockapoo because she will want to please you, and oh yes, she's not too fussy about treats either. When your puppy does something right, reward her immediately with a tempting treat, praising her at the same time with 'Yes' or 'Good dog' in a happy, encouraging voice.

In time, you can wean her from the food-based training and she will obey you purely for the fun of the training itself. But even then, you should reward her with treats intermittently.

When to start

Training starts the moment you bring your puppy home. Even if you've signed up for puppy classes at some future date, don't wait. Teach her what you can, little by little, moment by moment. Practice often, and never give up. When she's under six months, keep these sessions to no more than ten minutes at a time.

Who's responsible

Anyone and everyone in your puppy's close and extended family – and all using the same set of rules, spoken commands, hand signals and body language.

Where?

Start training in a quiet place with no outside distractions. A closed room is infinitely better than a park filled with people, other dogs and new and interesting smells.

What needs to be learned?

By the time she is six months old, your puppy should know her name and obey your orders to: 'Come', 'Sit' and 'Down'. She should also have been introduced to 'Stay'.

How?

All commands should be spoken clearly, firmly and with confidence. Lengthen the vowel sounds and make sure the consonants are crisp and clear.

And don't forget gestures. It might surprise you to learn that most dogs actually respond better to body language than words.

Finally it's also worth noting that, while it's important to be a clear leader to your puppy, there's no need to be dominant. Cockapoos already want to please you by doing what you ask of them.

NAME RECOGNITION

One of the first things your puppy needs to learn is to recognise her name. After all, how else will she know that you're communicating specifically with her?

Do

- From a short distance – three or four feet is fine – call her clearly, using her name just once.
- Use a happy, friendly voice.
- Crouch down if you can.
- Open your arms to welcome her (body language is hugely important).
- Make a fuss of her when she gets to you.
- If she doesn't respond, wait a few seconds then call again, still clearly, and still just the once.
- When she does come, praise her lovingly, give her a treat and tell her how brilliantly clever she is.
- Practise this often.

Don't

- Overuse her name or say it repeatedly in quick succession, or she will soon learn to ignore it.

EYE CONTACT

If your puppy's not looking at you, she's probably not listening either. Calling her name will encourage her to look at you and, when she does, you can know she's engaged. She's turning to you to find out what's coming next: will you open the door, take her for a walk, throw the ball? It's excellent that she's turning to you for answers and provision, so make sure you reward her.

CALLING HER TO YOU

If your puppy only knows one command it should be 'Come' or 'Here'. Coming to you when she's called is important for your relationship, and essential for her safety too. Recall is much like the name recognition exercise and now, while she's little, is a very good time to teach it to her because this is when she needs you more than ever for love, food and safety. In fact, if she's already joined your family, chances are she is with you right now, under your feet or helping you to absorb this book. Digest it even. And chances are she already relates the recall command to something fun and exciting: food, a new toy, or playtime.

Do

- Follow the steps in the Name Recognition exercise above, using her name and adding a calling word like 'Come' or 'Here'. Consistency is key, so choose whichever word you prefer and stick with it.
- Call her to you often, gradually increasing the initial distance between you.
- Practice at home and on a lead before you let her go when you are out and about.
- When you do let her off the lead away from home, make sure it is in a very safe place. Then practise letting her go and calling her back.
- If she keeps following you anyway, find someone who can help you by holding her while you back away. Then entice her, if necessary, and when she is struggling to get to you, your helper can let her go. Only then, when she is running to you, call her name and 'Come' or 'Here'.
- Your welcoming body language can be very helpful with this too. Try getting down on your haunches or your knees and opening your arms wide to greet her.

Don't

- If you call your puppy to you and she gets side-tracked en route, you might be tempted to scold her when she finally arrives. But coming to you should ALWAYS be associated with good things, so never punish her if she doesn't come straight away. If you do, she'll associate the scolding with the last thing she's done – come to you. Then, understandably from her point of view, next time you call her she might think twice about coming back at all. (See 'Timing is all-important' in the chapter on Behaviour.)

- Don't always put her back on a lead when she comes to you, or she will soon learn that coming means the end of her free-play session. Only put her back on the lead after several recalls.

TIP
If she develops the habit of running up to you but then dancing around just out of your reach, start withholding her treat until AFTER you have a grip on her collar.

'SIT'

This is one of the most useful exercises you can teach your puppy.

- Call her to you and hold a treat, palm facing down, just in front of her nose for her to smell.

- When you've got her interest, slowly take the treat up a couple of inches and over her head (slightly behind and above her eyes). If she jumps up and paws you, start again, keeping the treat even closer to her nose.
- When she lowers her bottom, and only then, say 'Sit!' and give her the treat.
- Once she is doing this well, you can move on to the next stage. Wait until her bottom is actually on the floor before you say 'Sit!', and then treat her.
- She will soon learn to associate the word with the action. In time she will sit after you've given the command, and you can teach her to sit for longer stretches, from further away and during distractions.

'DOWN'

- It is best to start teaching this command when your puppy is already in an attentive Sit.
- Without feeding her the treat in your hand, move your hand, still palm down, from above her nose and towards the floor, between her front paws and close to her body.
- When she lowers her nose and front paws, keeping her bottom on the ground, say 'Down!' in a clear voice and give her the treat.
- When she is doing this well, you can wait until her tummy and all four paws are flat on the floor before you say 'Down!', and only then give her the treat.

'STAY'

This is an essential command for your puppy's safety – or that of any dog that might dash out the front door, across a road, or leap out of the car.

The training involves teaching her to remain in a Sit or Down position for increasingly long times before you reward her.

- Once she is in a 'Sit' or a 'Down', say 'Stay!' in a strong but soothing voice, and combine this with a clear hand signal. Point to the ground just in front of her with your arm straight, your palm flat and your fingers together.
- If she gets up, simply ask for the Sit or Down position again and repeat the 'Stay' command.
- When she has stayed for a few seconds, say 'Good!' (or a 'release' word of your choice) and treat her.
- Gradually work up to longer times, but no more than 30 seconds, and step back in increments to increase the distance. (Try not to give her unrealistic goals; the idea is to push her to the limit while letting her succeed.)
- Keep her on a lead when you put this command into practice at the front door or in the car.

What if the training's 'not working'?

If your puppy doesn't do what you've asked (assuming she's not hard of hearing):

- she doesn't understand and needs clearer instructions,
- she needs more practice,
- or she needs a better reason to obey you – like a treat, an even better treat (squares of fresh chicken or liver. Yum!), or higher praise.

EXPANDING ON THE BASICS

Extension exercises

Duration – Once your puppy can do an exercise, like 'Sit' for example, you can gradually ask her to sit for longer periods before treating her.

Distractions – You can slowly increase the distractions too. A 'Sit' when a squirrel is taunting your puppy from a nearby tree is very different from a 'Sit' in a quiet place. Once she's mastered the instruction in a quiet room, start practicing it in a busier part of the house, then at the park, and so on.

Distance – In time, you can also begin asking your puppy to 'Sit' from slightly further away from you, but start with just a couple of steps and don't forget the all-important hand signals.

Advanced commands – If you'd like to add to these basic commands, your puppy can go on to learn 'Stand', 'Settle', 'Heel' and many more. There are some excellent obedience training guides on the market, and if training classes are available in your area, they are well worth the effort and your puppy would love you for taking her.

PATIENCE AND UNCONDITIONAL LOVE

Cockapoos are generally easier to train than most breeds, but they can put on some spectacular displays of selective hearing, so don't judge yourself harshly if your puppy misbehaves. Nobody said this was easy.

26. PLAYTIME!

Cockapoos absolutely **love** to play. Your puppy would spend every waking minute playing with you if you'd play along. And that's a good thing, because as well as contributing to the mental and physical exercise Cockapoos so badly need, playing helps with socialisation and improves communication skills. Most importantly of all, it's great fun. But whether this play is purely for fun or a more structured exercise, keep these 'Rules of Play' top of mind.

- Start playtimes when your puppy is being good, so you're not rewarding him for bad behaviour.
- Several short play sessions spread throughout the day are always better than one long one.
- Whatever games you're playing, remember he's only little, so don't overpower him. Aim to match your strength, speed and energy to his own.
- As far as possible, get down low to his level.

- If a toy is involved, avoid hard tugging. It puts pressure on his teeth and encourages more aggressive play. A good way to manage the pressure is to hold the toy by your fingertips.
- When your puppy wins the toy, encourage him back to teach him that playing is more about having fun together than possession.
- If the playing does shift from fun interaction to possession of a toy, then stop for a while.
- Always try to calm the playing down before you stop. It's disappointing stopping a game when it's at its most exciting.
- And always end playtime on a good note. If you've had to stop for a moment, restart the game and end it when things are quiet and friendly.
- Avoid exciting games just before his bedtime.

For playtime to be great fun, you really just need each other – there's no need for fancy toys or expensive equipment. Sharing a walk, throwing a ball or paddling in the shallows can be the most special times. But if you're still looking to expand your activities, here are some ideas.

GAMES

All puppies have their favourites and you'll soon figure out which ones you play best together.

Chase

This is excellent practice for encouraging your puppy to come to you.

1. Flick a treat across the floor.
2. Let him chase after it.

3. When he comes back for more, make eye contact and praise him.
4. Only then flick another treat across the floor, and so on.

Fetch

This is an extension of Chase, but played outside or in a much bigger space.

1. Throw things for him to fetch: toys, a ball, a treat.
2. Say 'Fetch!' as you throw each item.
3. Once he knows to fetch, start throwing the objects into harder-to-reach places.
4. If this doesn't work, throw more interesting toys or tastier treats.

Catch

You can play this with toys, treats and balls.

1. Start with something light and easy to grab hold of, like a floppy soft toy.
2. Throw it in an arc over his head, so that if he stayed in place it would land close to his muzzle.
3. If he misses, try to pick it up before he does and he'll soon learn that if he wants it he must catch it before it hits the ground.
4. When he's learned to catch, you can move on to balls as well. (Later he can progress to frisbees, but start off with a soft disc.)

Which hand?

1. With your hands behind your back, put a small treat or two in one hand and nothing in the other.
2. Make your hands into fists and bring them in front of you.

3. Let your puppy choose which fist he prefers the smell of.

4. When he's decided which hand he's interested in, and it's the right one, say 'Good!' and open your hand, letting him take the treat.

Treasure hunt

Your puppy will love this! Cockapoos excel at sniffing things out and relish any opportunity to put their skill to the test. What's more, rooting around for hidden treasure can be played just as well indoors as out.

1. The first time you play, let him watch as you hide a treat (something he can eat), then lead him away and say 'Find'.

2. Once he understands how the game works, you can make sure he can't see you when you hide the treat or a toy. Then lead him into the room or area where it's hidden, say 'Find', and this time he will have to follow your smell. (The first few times you might need to guide him.)

One day, when he is older and fully understands the game, you can make it more difficult by using 'Sit!' and 'Stay!' while you hide the treat, and then by hiding it in more difficult places too.

Obstacle course

1. Turn your passageway or garden into an obstacle course – build small jumps, make tunnels, fill a tea tray with water, arrange boxes to navigate around … anything you can think of that is safe.

2. Guide your puppy through the course and reward him with treats each time he overcomes an obstacle.

TOYS

The retriever in your puppy will have him parading his toys around like trophies, wagging madly and waiting for praise, no matter what he's 'found'. Nevertheless, look for variety when you're choosing his toys. You want to expose him to a range of experiences through objects that roll, bounce or squeak; things that are wonderfully chewy, or simply soft and cuddly.

Then, to keep him interested in his playthings, don't put them all out at once. Only let him play with or chew a few at a time, and rotate them through the week or even the day.

Presumably he'll already have a few simple toys, but here are three ideas to make his playtimes that little bit more interesting and challenging.

The maze

There are a number of 'slow feeders' on the market which are maze-like in design. These were originally intended for dogs who gulp their food down too fast, but they also work brilliantly for brain-training.

- Put a treat or two in the middle of the maze and let your puppy use his paws, nose and tongue to work them out before he can eat them. (Make sure you've chosen one suitable for his size so he can actually manage this.)

The hollow chew

Hollow toys made of hard rubber are available online and from most pet stores. The Kong is a great example; it comes in a range of sizes and is dishwasher safe. Fill one of these with small dog treats, or even with meat, marmite or peanut butter (as long as it contains no

Xylitol). Your puppy will spend hours trying to extract whatever you've filled it up with.

Treat-dispensing balls

There are plenty of treat-dispensing or 'activity' balls on the market in a range of shapes and sizes. Put dry food or treats inside one of these and your puppy will love rolling it around to get the pieces out.

EQUIPMENT

Use your imagination, but make sure whatever you come up with is safe, and well secured where necessary.

- Hay bales can be used as jumps, steps and passageways
- Old tires make fabulous jump hoops
- Children's paddling pools are great fun for playing in as well as cooling off in on hot days
- Look in children's toy stores – tunnels, playhouses and sand boxes will appeal to your puppy too.

27. TRAVELLING BY CAR

Of course your puppy would love nothing more than to stand on the front passenger seat, stick his head out the window and feel the wind in his face, but car travel is not the time for free play. He needs to be restrained so that he can't distract you while you're driving, or injure you or himself if you have to stop quickly. The restraint is also there to keep your insurance valid in the event of an accident.

Ideally you should invest in one of the following, depending on whether you want your puppy to travel on the back seats, or – if your car has a rear door – in the space behind the back seats:

- a seatbelt harness – well-padded and comfortable, that fastens securely into your vehicle's existing seatbelt fitting,
- a crate or cage that is small enough to fit in the back area of your car while also being big enough for your adult dog to sit up and have a stretch in,
- a dog guard – fitted between the back seats of your car and the trunk/boot area.

All of these are available in pet stores and online.

Do

- For everyone's safety, use a dog seatbelt, crate or cage, or dog guard.

- If you are using a seat belt, always attach your dog by his harness, never a collar.
- Whenever you are getting him into the car or letting him out, make sure it is on the pavement side of the road and never the side with the traffic.
- For his own safety, teach him to 'Stay!' in the car until he is given a release command.
- On long journeys, stop regularly to let him relieve himself and stretch his legs. These stops will also help ease any car sickness he might experience.
- If it's a sunny day and he's in a travel crate or strapped in, make sure he's on the shady side of the car. Being stuck in blaring sunlight would hurt him even more than it would you.

Never

- Allow your puppy or dog on your lap while you're driving. He must always be restrained.
- Allow him on the front passenger seat, especially if an airbag is fitted.
- Tie him in place on the back seat by his collar and lead instead of using a proper seatbelt harness.
- Leave him unattended in a hot or even warm car. Not even for a few minutes. Dog fatalities from heatstroke in cars are frighteningly common.

28. PUPPY-PEOPLE TRANSLATOR

Your dog understands your every word, or so it's said. The point is, your choice of words is very important. Even more important though is **how** you say them. Be clear in your speech and body language and be gentle but firm, patient, loving, encouraging, reassuring.

It is also said that a dog can say more with her tail in just a few seconds than her owner can say in hours. If she's already in your life, you will be familiar with her favourite expressions: 'I am so happy to see you!' and 'You're the best thing that ever happened to me!' In her first days with you, you will no doubt have experienced, 'Your face is like a lovely lolly!' And before long, you could be surprised when she lets you know that: 'Your training is coming along very nicely!'

Yup, a lot of your puppy's body language is really easy to read, but truth be told the signs are not always straightforward. How good are you really at understanding her language and feelings? By way of example, a wagging tail can be a sign of happiness as well as one of aggression, so we need to look at the whole picture, including: how she wags it, what the rest of her body is doing at the time and what else is going on around her.

To help with this, here are some Puppy-People translations:

I love you

- Racing to meet you
- Wagging tail
- Licking
- Whimpering

I'm happy and excited

- Tail wagging fast (but watch out as this can also be a sign of concentration or aggression)
- Racing around
- Whimpering
- Pulling lips back and exposing teeth

Let's play

- Wagging tail vigorously
- Rolling head
- Dashing off and jumping back again
- Jumping in front of you, facing you, front legs splayed out
- Elbows on the ground and bottom in the air
- Bounding leaps and running in circles
- Lying down or rolling over
- Barking intermingled with growls (can be confused with aggression)

What is that I hear? Where is it coming from?

- One paw raised
- Head tilted to the side
- Brow raised
- Ears twitch and nose wiggles
- Mouth may be open and panting

Totally chilled out

- Lying on back with legs flopped out
- Curled in a ball
- Lying down watching you

Feeling submissive

- Rolling over onto back, exposing tummy and genitals
- Tail between legs
- Head dipped or tucked in, ears pinned back

I'm curious, and maybe a little concerned, about something going on out there

- Raised paw

I'm frightened or unhappy

- Tail between legs
- Cowering, or lying down
- Ears twitching back and forth
- Staring ahead at object of fear
- Lying down with paws ahead, looking ahead, ready to run
- Raised hackles (hairs along the top of her back). Can be tricky to spot in a fluffy Cockapoo coat.
- Whining or whimpering
- Looking to you for help

I'm in pain or frightened and want your help

- Looking from you to whatever it is she needs, and then quickly back again
- Whining or whimpering
    This is not manipulation. It's a genuine plea for help. Tell her you're there for her and she can count on you.

Feeling aggressive

- Standing up straight
- Ears pinned back, or sharply forward
- Hackles raised
- Low growl with eyes fixed in a direct stare
- Body tense, ready to attack
- Tail held stiffly, or wagging in stiff, quick, stilted movements
- Barking
- Lunging at other people or dogs
- Snarling, growling or biting (usually in defence of you, food, toys or territory, or copying another dog)

I'm warning you

- Snarling or growling
- Baring fangs

Feeling lonely and locating other dogs, or sending out a warning

- Howling
- Baying

I want your attention: 'hello', 'look at me', 'I'm bored'

- Barking directly at you

I'm begging you. Pleeez!

- Whining, with pleading eyes

    Yes, it's a heart-wrenching expression, but don't give in to that endearing face. Your environment will help you to tell the difference between manipulative begging and 'I'm in pain or frightened and need your help'. If you're eating a juicy sausage that she's hoping you'll share, it's fairly safe to assume she's begging.

29. ADOLESCENCE

Around six months, your puppy will begin chewing her relentless path through adolescence which is usually the most difficult period for owners. Her newfound independence and low tolerance for boredom will bring an increased interest in exploring, chewing, digging and all manner of relationship-testing behaviour. Hopefully the solid foundations you've laid in the early weeks and months will make this phase a little less wearing. Remind yourself it is short-lived.

Running off

During adolescence, your puppy's love of exploring will reach new heights and she could start running off. If she does, it's most likely because she (or he) is at the onset of sexual maturity and wants to mate, and if this behaviour persists, prevention is always the better option. At home you will need to keep her inside or in a fully enclosed garden or yard, and while walking out she will need to stay on the lead.

But if she does run off, be sure to praise her when she comes back. Never scold her when she gets to you, because in coming back she is being a good puppy. That way she will want to stay with you (or home) and, even if she does run off again, she will always want to return.

Sexual maturity

Somewhere between six months and a year, your little girl, if that's what you have, will come into season and be overcome with the urge to roam. Your little boy could begin mounting things and showing aggression towards other male dogs. Both sexes, if un-neutered (meaning they haven't been spayed or castrated) might begin marking their territory by urinating. Basically both sexes will experience hormonal changes that are likely to affect their behaviour, so if you're not considering breeding, you will be faced with the important question of neutering.

NEUTERING

Although neutering is likely to reduce bad behaviours in time, it won't solve your puppy issues, either completely or overnight. But your puppy's health and wellbeing are important factors here too. This is in fact a highly controversial subject and beyond the parameters of this book. Most vets and breeders consider neutering the more responsible option, but to help you decide here are some of the key pros and cons.

Neutering your female dog

(also referred to as spaying or de-sexing)

Advantages:

- It prevents unwanted pregnancies,
- stops her from coming into season (into heat), which involves a period of bleeding every six months or so, lasting anything from two to four weeks,
- reduces hormone-associated mood swings, including possible anxiety and aggression towards other dogs,

- stops her from trying to escape to find a mate,
- keeps persistent male dogs from pursuing her during her season,
- dispels the need for weeks of lockdown. (A female in season should never be left outdoors unattended, even in a secured area, and must be kept on a lead when out on walks),
- reduces territory marking by urinating,
- reduces the risk of a number of health problems, including infections of the uterus and ovarian and mammary cancers.

Disadvantages:

- It involves major surgery (removing the ovaries and uterus),
- increases the risk of obesity,
- increases the chance of urinary incontinence,
- might affect the silky quality of her coat.

Neutering your male dog

(also referred to as castrating or de-sexing)

Advantages:

- It prevents accidental breeding,
- lessens dominance and aggression,
- cuts back on undesirable sexual behaviour, such as inappropriate mounting,
- reduces leg lifting and territorial urine marking,
- lowers the urge to run off after females in season,
- minimises the risk of attack by other males,
- reduces the risk of a number of health problems, including prostate disorders and testicular cancer.

Disadvantages of neutering:

- It involves surgery (removal of the testicles),
- increases the risk of obesity,

- increases the risk of a number of health problems, including bone cancer if done before a year, and joint problems if done before six months,
- might affect the silky quality of his coat.

When to neuter

The best age for neutering is also open to debate.

Some vets advise operating as early as four months of age, while others won't consider neutering before six. With females, some vets recommend neutering before your puppy's first season, while others argue that she should have had at least one season, or even a litter of puppies. With males, some vets will operate any time from eight weeks, as long as both testicles have descended; some recommend neutering after six months but before nine to help curb dominant male behaviours; and others recommend waiting longer.

Then again, many recent studies suggest that neutering too early can result in emotional and behavioural problems, and argue for waiting until your puppy/dog has reached physical as well as emotional maturity. Physically, the average Cockapoo will reach its full adult height by a year, but its bones are developing up until around 18 months, and it can continue filling out and gaining muscle until it is two. Emotional maturity is more difficult to pinpoint, but less bounce and reduced chewing are both good indicators.

So it seems the recommended age lies in the unhelpfully wide range of between four and 18 months. But discuss this with your own vet as well as other Cockapoo owners if you can, because this is an important consideration.

30. GOING FORWARD

This book sets out to answer the most important early-stage questions on owning a Cockapoo puppy. It covers the things you need to know when he is still very young – the things you don't want to get wrong in his vital first months. Now here are a few key things to be aware or reminded of as he blossoms into adulthood.

Fear period

As if adolescence isn't tricky enough, it's possible that between seven and eight months your puppy could experience another fear period. Of course you're unlikely to know for sure, but to be on the safe side, prepare yourself with saint-like gentleness, patience and understanding.

The special place

When your puppy is toilet trained and has stopped eating everything in sight, you will be able to start leaving the door to his crate or special space open. In the meantime, remember to keep praising him when you see him going in there on his own.

Food

It is your job to manage his food intake and keep a check on his weight; extra weight puts unnecessary strain on his joints and organs. You should be able to feel his ribs below the surface of his skin, without much padding, so check this regularly and if you do notice that his weight is creeping up – and this is especially likely after neutering – immediately cut back on the treats.

As a reminder, between eight and twelve months you might want to move him on to a 'junior' formula, but don't progress to 'adult' food until he is over a year.

Exercise

From nine months to a year, and as an adult, your Cockapoo should ideally be getting a good 45 minutes' to an hour's exercise morning and evening. If he shows signs of boredom, hyperactivity or starts putting on weight, you can increase this.

When he's fully grown, he could make a great hiking partner if you want to head for the hills, but build up the distances slowly. He could make a fabulous running companion too but, as with the walking, you would need to work up the distances slowly. With both walking and running, be mindful of his paws, staying away from long stretches of hard ground and surfaces that might be very hot, or cold and icy.

Swimming is fantastic exercise in the long term. It's

low impact and easy on the joints. But remember that it's more tiring than walking or running, and that it's up to you to call an end to his swim sessions.

Nails

Apart from being uncomfortable, nails that are too long can cause splayed feet and lameness. Some very active Cockapoos never need their nails clipped, but most do. You can tell they need a trim if his toes splay apart, or his nails scratch the ground when he's standing upright. Better still, check them as part of his regular grooming routine, clipping or filing tiny bits at every bath time or trimming session.

If your Cockapoo has dew claws – the nails on the upper insides of his feet – remember that these need trimming too to prevent them from catching on things or growing into the skin.

Collar

Keep up the checks on his collar, loosening it whenever it becomes too tight.

Tying up

Absolutely not. Please don't ever tie up your puppy out in the garden or yard. It's unthinkable that if you're reading this book you would consider this an option. I know you won't, but it's still worth mentioning that leaving any dog tied up like that would make him frustrated, deeply unhappy and even neurotic. Sanity aside, it would put him at risk of hurting his neck or choking; prevent him from escaping from unpredictable danger, such as other dogs, fire or flooding; or simply from finding shelter from frightening situations like loud bangs, or thunder and lightning.

Fine tuning

At a later stage you might well choose to fine-tune your training, or need to deal with specific behavioural issues that might've arisen. There are some excellent and extremely thorough books on the market.

And if you've got the time and inclination for obedience training or agility classes – any competition that challenges him physically and mentally – they are incredibly enriching for both you and your dog, and he would love you all the more for taking him.

31. THERE WILL BE TIMES ...

This book is intended as an easy read to offer you some shortcuts with the theory. But there are NO shortcuts with the practice. The practice needs patience and repetition, encouragement and reward.

Tough times

There will be times when your puppy does all sorts of things you don't want her to. When she's bored and teething, she will set her alligator jaws to work, chomping their happy way through your designer chairs. She will gift you with shredded items of now ex-value, and with random deposits of unidentifiable bodily waste.

She will slop her muddy paws across your cream-coloured carpet, then wait until she's well and truly indoors before shaking off the rest of the mud. She will bark when she has something to say, and whine when she's upset or lonely.

For months, your house will be littered with toys, and the tick-tack of little paws will be under your feet when you go to the fridge, the toilet, the shower and the front door.

There will be many times when you're at your wits' end and you will look at her and think, 'What **have** I got myself into?'

Good times

Well it's this: you have a new family member who will bowl you over with her bounding love, drape her

teddy-bear self over your best furniture, pull at your heartstrings with her soft, pleading eyes, and test your sense of humour with her tireless antics.

But it's precisely because of the boundless energy and unrelenting enthusiasm, the soft-fluffy feel, the velcro-adoration and the endless blundering capers that we love these dogs so much. So remember that when you feel your patience running thin. And no matter how often your Cockapoo seems like a small child covered in fur, don't try to make her more human. Just as she is, she will give you more love and more fun than you could ever imagine, and there will be many times when you ask yourself, 'How **did** I get so lucky?'

Your family has grown by four furry feet and when you get home, your puppy's wet nose, sparkling eyes and wiggle-bottom tail wait to greet you, ecstatic to see you. She will melt your heart, bring you buckets of laughs and enrich your life with her eagerness to please and unconditional love.

There will also be plenty of times when she does the things you DO want her to do. Praise her – with attention, treats, toys … it doesn't matter what, as long as it's something she loves.

Taking-her-for-granted times

And last, but definitely not least, there will be times when she just IS – a calm, quiet presence by your side. Those are the times when it will be easiest for you to forget or ignore her, and those are the times when it is most important of all to remind yourself, and her, just how special she is.

32. USEFUL CONTACTS

All About Dog Food
www.allaboutdogfood.co.uk

American Canine Hybrid Club
www.achclub.com

American Cockapoo Club
www.americancockapooclub.com

Breeders Online
www.breedersonline.co.uk

British Cockapoo Society
www.britishcockapoosociety.com

Cockapoo Club of America
www.cockapooclub.com

Dog Food Advisor (product reviews and ratings)
www.dogfoodadvisor.com

International Designer Canine Registry (IDCR)
designercanineregistry.com

The Cockapoo Club of Great Britain (the official registration body for Cockapoos)
www.cockapooclubgb.co.uk

The Cockapoo Owners Club UK
www.cockapooowners-club.org.uk

The Doodle Trust (UK-wide charity for the rehoming of Poodle crossbreeds)
www.doodletrust.com

INDEX

Adolescence 10, 157-160

Adult/hood 161-164

Adverts 37

Aggression 29, 80, 154, 156, 158

Agility 164

Allergies 89

Alone 121

American Cockapoo Club 24-25

American Cocker Spaniel 19-20

Ancestry 12, 17-24, 29-30, 33

Anti-chew 51, 54

Barking 80, 117-120, 154, 156

Basket (see Bed)

Bathing (see Washing)

Bed 49, 68, 101

Begging 90, 156

Behaviour 97-103, 158

Bell training 106

Bite/biting 111, 156

Blanket 38, 42, 46. 49, 56

Body language 101, 138, 153-156

Bones 64, 130, 132

Bowls 50, 59

Boy (see Male)

Breed standard 24-25

Breeder 31-38, 42, 56

Brushing (see Grooming)

Call (see Come)

Cars 52, 151-152

Catch 147

Cats 62-63, 118

Characteristics 12-16

Chew/ing 108-110, 157

Chews 51

Children 62, 80-81, 112

Chocolate 64

Clipping 15, 94

Clubs 24, 32, 34

Coat 15, 18, 21, 25, 27

Cockapoo Club of Great Britain 24

Cocker Spaniel 12, 13, 17-20, 27

Collar 50, 56, 73, 85, 152

Colouring 21, 27-28

Come 139-141

Communication 84, 136, 145

Coprophagia (see Poo eating)

Cost 16, 35, 37

Crate 49, 52, 60, 82, 101

Crossbreed 7, 12, 17-24, 39

Dangers (see Safe/ty)
Deposit 46
Dew claws 95, 163
Deworming 34, 39, 40, 74
Digging 115-116
Docking (Tails) 25
Dominance 43-46
Down (lying) 142
Ears 25, 43, 91-92, 133, 154
Encourage 69-70, 97-98
English Cocker Spaniels 19-20
Exercise 13, 83, 85, 124, 130-135, 162-163
Eye contact 139
Eyes 25, 40, 43
F numbers (eg F1, F2b) 23-24, 33
Fear 75, 80, 119, 155, 161
Feeding (see Food)
Female 28-29, 158-159
Fetch 147
Fireworks 78
First night 66-68
Fleas 96
Food 46, 50, 56, 60, 71-72, 86-90, 162
Games 146-148
Gates (dog/baby/stair gates) 52, 61

Generation (see F numbers)
Girl (see Female)
Grass seeds 134
Grooming 15, 52, 90-96
Growling 154, 156
Guarantee 36, 41
Habituation 77
Hackles 155, 156
Handling 70
Harness 50, 56, 125-129, 152
Health 23, 34, 43, 55
Health clearance (see Paperwork)
Hearing 15
Heat (in season) 29, 158-160
Heat (temperature) 82, 85-86, 124, 152
Here (see Come)
Hot water bottle 52, 66
House training (see Toilet training)
Independence 44, 70-71
Inoculation (see Vaccination)
Insurance 47, 57, 74
Jumping up 113-114
Kennel Club 19, 24
Lead 50, 125-129
Leader 84, 100

Lifespan 10, 35
Litter 22, 26, 33, 42
Litter mates 44, 111, 113
Male 28-29, 159-160
Marking territory 29, 158, 159
Markings 27-28
Meal/s (see Food)
Microchip 35, 39, 40, 74
Miniature Poodle 21-22
Mother 33, 34, 42, 56
Mounting 158
Mouthing 111-112
Movement 25
Nails 74, 94-95, 163
Name 53, 70, 138-139
Neutering 29, 158-162
Nipping 111-112
Noise 78, 124
Nose 43
Odour eliminator 52, 106
Older dog 10
Other dogs 11, 58-59, 62, 118, 128
Other pets 11, 62-63
Paperwork 35, 39-41, 42, 56
Parasites 96
Pedigree 24, 39, 41
Pick-up day 54-57
Plants 48-49, 134
Play pen 52

Playing/Playtime 72, 84, 128, 132, 145-150
Poisonous 47-49
Poo eating 82-83
Poodle 8, 12, 18, 21-22, 26, 27, 40
Poo/p bags 51, 128
Potty training (see Toilet training)
Preparation 47-53
Puppy dealers 32, 37
Puppy farmers (see Puppy dealers)
Puppy-proofing (see Safe/ty)
Purebred 24
Quick (of nails) 95
Quiet time (see Time alone)
Recall (see Come)
Re-homing 10
Reputable/responsible breeders 31-38
Retrievers 108
Rules 52-53, 69, 101, 145-146
Running 132, 162
Running off 157
Safety 47-49, 61-65, 77-78, 127-129, 133-135
Sales contract 41, 46
Season (see Heat)

Separation anxiety 12, 79, 116, 121-124
Shedding 14, 18, 27
'Show' Cocker Spaniel 19
Sit 89, 141-142
Size 21-22, 25, 26
Sleep 60, 66-68
Smell/s 38
Snow 134
Socialisation 76, 145
Spaying (see Neutering)
Standard Poodle 21-22, 30, 107
Stay 89, 143, 152
Sticks 109
Submissive 43-46, 107, 155
Swimming 92, 132-133, 162-163
Tag (ID) 50
Tail 25, 153-156
Teeth 95, 108
Teething 108, 110, 111
Temperament 13, 15, 28, 43
Temperature (see Heat)
Temptation 65, 99
Theft 86
Ticks 96
Time alone 73, 79, 85

Timing 30-31, 101-102
Toilet training 60, 68, 72, 104-107
Toy Poodle 21-22, 30, 107, 121
Toys 51, 122-123, 149-150
Training 136-144
Travel 56-57, 151-152
Treats 50-51, 60, 90, 98, 108, 137
Trimming (see Nails or Clipping)
Tying up 163
Vaccinations 35, 39, 40, 59, 74, 77, 125
Vet 32, 47, 74, 160
Walks/Stepping out 125-129, 130-132
Washing 92-93
Water (drinking) 60, 71, 86
Water (other) 16, 47, 61, 132
Weight 25, 89-90, 162
Whining/Whimpering 154-156
'Working' Cocker Spaniel 19-20, 30
Worms (see Deworming)
Xylitol 64, 150

Printed in Great Britain
by Amazon

63729607R00099